Better Homes and Gardens®

all-time-favorite
Barbecue
recipes

Better Homes and Gardens® Books
Des Moines, Iowa

All of us at Better Homes and Gardens₀ Books are dedicated to providing you with the information and ideas you need to create delicious foods. We welcome your comments and suggestions. Write to us at:

Better Homes and Gardens₀ Books
Cookbook Editorial Department
1716 Locust St.
Des Moines, IA 50309-3023

If you would like to purchase any of our books, check wherever quality books are sold.
Visit our website at bhg.com

Our seal assures you that every recipe in *all-time-favorite Barbecue recipes* has been tested in the Better Homes and Gardens₀ Test Kitchen. This means that each recipe is practical and reliable, and meets our high standards of taste appeal. We guarantee your satisfaction with this book for as long as you own it.

Shown on the cover:
Steaks with Blue Cheese Butter
(recipe, page 35)

Better Homes and Gardens₀ Books
An imprint of Meredith₀ Books

all-time-favorite Barbecue recipes
Editor: Carrie Holcomb Mills
Contributing Editors: Spectrum Communication Services, Inc.
Art Director: Conyers Design, Inc.
Designer: Sundie Ruppert
Photographers: Jim Krantz, Kritsada Panichgul
Food Stylists: Janet Pittman, Dianna Nolin
Illustrator: Chad Johnston
Indexer: Sharon Duffy
Copy and Production Editor: Terri Fredrickson
Contributing Proofreaders: Gretchen Kaufmann, Susan J. Kling
Electronic Production Coordinator: Paula Forest
Editorial and Design Assistants: Judy Bailey, Mary Lee Gavin, Karen Schirm
Test Kitchen Director: Lynn Blanchard
Production Manager: Pam Kvitne, Marjorie J. Schenkelberg

Meredith₀ Books
Editor in Chief: James D. Blume
Design Director: Matt Strelecki
Managing Editor: Gregory H. Kayko
Executive Food Editor: Jennifer Dorland Darling

Director, Retail Sales and Marketing: Terry Unsworth
Director, Sales, Special Markets: Rita McMullen
Director, Sales, Premiums: Michael A. Peterson
Director, Sales, Retail: Tom Wierzbicki
Director, Book Marketing: Brad Elmitt
Director, Operations: George A. Susral
Director, Production: Douglas M. Johnston

Vice President, General Manager: Jamie L. Martin

Better Homes and Gardens₀ Magazine
Editor in Chief: Jean LemMon
Executive Food Editor: Nancy Byal

Meredith Publishing Group
President, Publishing Group: Stephen M. Lacy
Vice President, Finance and Administration: Max Runciman

Meredith Corporation
Chairman and Chief Executive Officer: William T. Kerr

Chairman of the Executive Committee: E. T. Meredith III

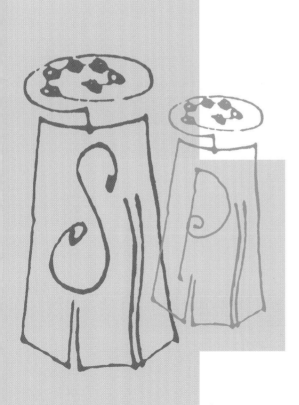

contents

chicken & turkey

Sticky-Sloppy Barbecue Chicken
(recipe, page 6)

sticky-sloppy barbecue chicken

Country meets city in this finger-licking barbecue recipe. Sherry supplies the uptown flavor. (Recipe pictured on pages 4-5.)

1½ cups dry sherry

1 cup finely chopped onion

¼ cup lemon juice

6 cloves garlic, minced

2 bay leaves

3 to 4 pounds meaty chicken pieces (breasts, thighs, and drumsticks)

1 15-ounce can tomato puree

¼ cup honey

3 tablespoons molasses

1 teaspoon salt

½ teaspoon dried thyme, crushed

¼ to ½ teaspoon ground red pepper

¼ teaspoon black pepper

2 tablespoons white vinegar

For Marinade: In a medium mixing bowl stir together sherry, onion, lemon juice, garlic, and bay leaves. Set aside.

To Prepare Poultry: Place chicken in a plastic bag set in a deep bowl. Pour marinade over chicken in bag. Seal bag and turn chicken to coat well. Marinate in the refrigerator for 2 to 4 hours, turning bag occasionally. Drain chicken, reserving marinade. Cover and chill chicken until ready to use.

For Sauce: In a large saucepan combine the reserved marinade, the tomato puree, honey, molasses, salt, thyme, red pepper, and black pepper. Bring to boiling; reduce heat. Simmer, uncovered, about 30 minutes or until reduced to 2 cups. Remove from heat; remove bay leaves. Stir in vinegar.

To Cook by Indirect Grill Method: In a covered grill arrange preheated coals around a drip pan. Test for medium heat above the pan. Place chicken, bone side down, on grill rack over the drip pan. Cover and grill for 50 to 60 minutes or until chicken is tender and no longer pink, brushing with some of the sauce during the last 15 minutes of grilling.

To Serve: Reheat and pass the remaining sauce with chicken. Makes 6 servings.

Nutrition Facts per serving: 446 cal., 13 g total fat (4 g sat. fat), 104 mg chol., 735 mg sodium, 33 g carbo., 35 g pro.

tandoori chicken

In India, this popular poultry dish is cooked in special ovens called tandoors. Your backyard grill and a spicy yogurt marinade replicate the traditional flavor.

1 8-ounce carton plain yogurt

1 tablespoon lemon juice

2 teaspoons grated fresh ginger or
    $^3/_4$ teaspoon ground ginger

1 teaspoon ground coriander

$^1/_2$ teaspoon ground cumin

$^1/_4$ teaspoon ground turmeric

$^1/_8$ teaspoon ground red pepper

1 clove garlic, minced

4 whole chicken breasts (about
    $1^1/_2$ pounds total), halved
    lengthwise

For Marinade: In a small mixing bowl combine yogurt, lemon juice, ginger, coriander, cumin, turmeric, red pepper, and garlic.

To Prepare Poultry: If desired, remove skin from chicken. Place chicken in a plastic bag set into a deep bowl. Pour marinade over chicken in bag. Seal bag and turn chicken to coat well. Marinate in the refrigerator for 6 to 24 hours, turning bag occasionally. Remove chicken from bag; discard marinade.

To Cook by Indirect Grill Method: In a covered grill arrange preheated coals around a drip pan. Test for medium heat above the pan. Place chicken, bone side down, on the grill rack over the drip pan. Cover and grill for 50 to 60 minutes or until chicken is tender and no longer pink. Makes 4 servings.

Nutrition Facts per serving: 224 cal., 8 g total fat (3 g sat. fat), 81 mg chol., 106 mg sodium, 6 g carbo., 31 g pro.

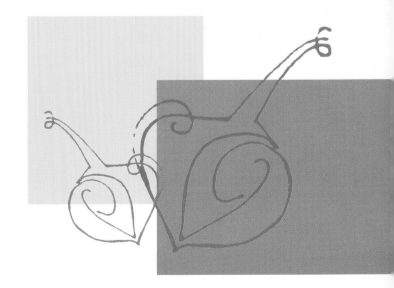

sizzling sesame chicken with vegetables

Grilled sweet red pepper and zucchini strips complement the sesame flavor of this Oriental-style chicken. If desired, remove the skin from the chicken before grilling.

1/2   cup chicken broth

  3   tablespoons soy sauce

  2   teaspoons toasted sesame oil

  1   teaspoon cornstarch

  1   teaspoon sugar

  1   clove garlic, minced

  1   tablespoon sesame seed

  2   pounds meaty chicken pieces (breasts, thighs, and drumsticks)

  1   large red or green sweet pepper, cut into 1-inch strips

  1   medium zucchini, halved crosswise and cut into 3×1-inch strips

For Sauce: In a small saucepan combine chicken broth, soy sauce, toasted sesame oil, cornstarch, sugar, and garlic. Cook and stir until thickened and bubbly. Cook and stir for 2 minutes more. Stir in sesame seed. Remove from heat; set aside.

To Cook by Indirect Grill Method: In a covered grill arrange preheated coals around a drip pan. Test for medium heat above the pan. Place chicken, bone side down, on the grill rack over the drip pan. Cover and grill for 50 to 60 minutes or until chicken is tender and no longer pink, brushing frequently with sauce the last 10 minutes of grilling. Place the pepper and zucchini beside the chicken perpendicular to the wires on the grill rack for the last 15 minutes of grilling, brushing occasionally with sauce.

To Cook by Direct Grill Method: Place chicken, bone side up, on the grill rack of an uncovered grill. Grill directly over medium coals for 35 to 45 minutes or until chicken is tender and no longer pink, turning once halfway through grilling time and brushing frequently with sauce the last 10 minutes of grilling. Place the pepper and zucchini beside the chicken perpendicular to the wires on the grill rack for the last 10 minutes of grilling, brushing occasionally with sauce. Makes 4 servings.

Nutrition Facts per serving: 308 cal., 16 g total fat (4 g sat. fat), 104 mg chol., 961 mg sodium, 5 g carbo., 35 g pro.

sesame-gingered barbecued chicken

What do the Orient and the Occident have in common? Well, a love of good barbecue, for one thing. This sweet-and-sour-hoisin-ginger-sesame sauce will please all palates.

¹/₃ cup plum sauce or sweet-and-sour sauce

¹/₄ cup water

3 tablespoons hoisin sauce

1¹/₂ teaspoons sesame seed (toasted, if desired)

1 teaspoon grated fresh ginger or ¹/₄ teaspoon ground ginger

1 clove garlic, minced

¹/₄ to ¹/₂ teaspoon Oriental chili sauce or several dashes bottled hot pepper sauce

6 medium skinless, boneless chicken breast halves and/or thighs (about 1¹/₂ pounds total)

For Sauce: In a small saucepan combine plum sauce, water, hoisin sauce, sesame seed, ginger, garlic, and Oriental chili sauce. Bring to boiling over medium heat, stirring frequently; reduce heat. Simmer, covered, for 3 minutes. Remove from heat.

To Cook by Direct Grill Method: Place chicken on the grill rack of an uncovered grill. Grill directly over medium coals for 12 to 15 minutes or until chicken is tender and no longer pink, turning once and brushing once or twice with some of the sauce the last 5 minutes of grilling.

To Serve: Reheat and pass the remaining sauce with chicken. Makes 6 servings.

Nutrition Facts per serving: *166 cal., 4 g total fat (1 g sat. fat), 59 mg chol., 216 mg sodium, 9 g carbo., 22 g pro.*

basil-and-garlic-stuffed chicken breasts

Simplify dinnertime chores—pound, roll, and stuff the chicken breasts ahead of time. Then, chill the rolled breasts until you are ready to grill them.

1/4 cup grated Parmesan cheese

2 to 3 tablespoons snipped fresh basil or 2 teaspoons dried basil, crushed

1 tablespoon margarine or butter, melted

2 cloves garlic, minced

4 skinless, boneless chicken breast halves (about 1 pound total)

1/2 teaspoon finely shredded lemon peel

2 tablespoons lemon juice

1 tablespoon margarine or butter, melted

For Stuffing: In a small mixing bowl combine Parmesan cheese, basil, 1 tablespoon margarine or butter, and the garlic. Set aside.

To Prepare Poultry: Place each breast half between 2 pieces of plastic wrap. Working from the center of the edges, pound lightly with the flat side of a meat mallet to 1/8-inch thickness. Remove plastic wrap. Spread stuffing on chicken. Fold in sides of each chicken breast; roll up jelly-roll style, pressing edges to seal. Fasten with wooden toothpicks.

For Sauce: In a small mixing bowl combine lemon peel, lemon juice, and 1 tablespoon margarine or butter.

To Cook by Indirect Grill Method: In a covered grill arrange preheated coals around a drip pan. Test for medium heat above the pan. Place chicken on the grill rack over the drip pan. Cover and grill for 20 to 25 minutes or until chicken is tender and no longer pink, brushing occasionally with sauce the last 10 minutes of grilling.

To Cook by Direct Grill Method: Place chicken on the grill rack of an uncovered grill. Grill directly over medium coals for 18 to 20 minutes or until chicken is tender and no longer pink, turning once halfway through grilling time and brushing occasionally with sauce the last 10 minutes of grilling. Makes 4 servings.

Nutrition Facts per serving: 205 cal., 11 g total fat (3 g sat. fat), 64 mg chol., 238 mg sodium, 2 g carbo., 24 g pro.

herbed-mustard chicken quarters

Another time, brush this oregano-scented sauce on pork chops.

1 tablespoon snipped parsley

1 tablespoon water

1 tablespoon mayonnaise or salad dressing

1 tablespoon Dijon-style mustard

1 teaspoon dried oregano, crushed

1/8 teaspoon ground red pepper

1 2$\frac{1}{2}$- to 3-pound broiler-fryer chicken, cut into quarters

For Sauce: In a small bowl combine parsley, water, mayonnaise, or salad dressing, Dijon-style mustard, oregano, and red pepper. Cover and refrigerate sauce until ready to use.

To Prepare Poultry: If desired, remove skin from the chicken.

To Cook by Indirect Grill Method: In a covered grill arrange preheated coals around a drip pan. Test for medium heat above the pan. Place chicken, bone side down, on the grill rack over the drip pan. Cover and grill for 50 to 60 minutes or until chicken is tender and no longer pink, brushing occasionally with sauce the last 10 minutes of grilling.

To Cook by Direct Grill Method: Place chicken, bone side up, on the grill rack of an uncovered grill. Grill directly over medium coals for 40 to 50 minutes or until chicken is tender and no longer pink, turning once halfway through grilling time and brushing occasionally with sauce the last 10 minutes of grilling. Makes 4 servings.

Nutrition Facts per serving: 297 cal., 18 g total fat (5 g sat. fat), 100 mg chol., 206 mg sodium, 1 g carbo., 31 g pro.

tips from the kitchen

is it done yet? The safest way to judge the doneness of meat is to use a meat thermometer. When using a thermometer, insert it into the thickest part of the food, making sure it isn't touching any bones, fat, or gristle. Take the meat off the grill when it has reached the minimum temperature. Remember, food continues to cook for several minutes after being removed from the grill and can become overcooked if not removed promptly. The internal temperature will rise about 5 degrees with standing.

grilled cajun chicken salad

Toss bits of peppery chicken with fresh-from-the-garden greens and vegetables.

$^1/_4$ cup salad oil

$^1/_4$ cup vinegar

1 tablespoon sugar

1 tablespoon snipped fresh thyme or $^1/_2$ teaspoon dried thyme, crushed

$^1/_4$ teaspoon dry mustard

1 tablespoon salad oil

1 teaspoon onion powder

$^1/_2$ teaspoon black pepper

$^1/_4$ teaspoon salt

$^1/_4$ teaspoon ground red pepper

4 skinless, boneless chicken breast halves (about 1 pound total)

4 cups torn mixed greens

1 medium carrot, shredded

$^1/_4$ cup sliced and halved radishes

1 green onion, sliced (2 tablespoons)

For Dressing: In a screw-top jar combine ¼ cup salad oil, vinegar, sugar, thyme, and mustard. Cover and shake well. Chill until serving time.

For Sauce: In a small mixing bowl combine 1 tablespoon salad oil, onion powder, black pepper, salt, and red pepper. Set aside.

To Cook by Indirect Grill Method: In a covered grill arrange preheated coals around a drip pan. Test for medium heat above the pan. Place chicken on the grill rack over the drip pan. Brush with half of the sauce. Cover and grill for 15 to 18 minutes or until chicken is tender and no longer pink, brushing occasionally with the remaining sauce.

To Cook by Direct Grill Method: Place chicken on the grill rack of an uncovered grill. Brush with half of the sauce. Grill directly over medium coals for 12 to 15 minutes or until chicken is tender and no longer pink, turning once and brushing occasionally with the remaining sauce.

To Serve: In a large salad bowl combine greens, carrot, radishes, and green onion. Cut chicken into bite-size pieces. Add chicken and dressing to salad. Toss to mix. Makes 4 servings.

Nutrition Facts per serving: *305 cal., 20 g total fat (3 g sat. fat), 59 mg chol., 219 mg sodium, 8 g carbo., 23 g pro.*

northwest chicken salad

1/4 cup pear nectar

2 tablespoons salad oil

2 tablespoons raspberry vinegar

1 teaspoon Dijon-style mustard

1 teaspoon toasted sesame oil

1 teaspoon dried basil, crushed

1/8 teaspoon black pepper

2 medium skinless, boneless chicken breast halves

10 thick asparagus spears, trimmed

4 cups shredded mixed salad greens

6 to 8 strawberries

1 pear, cored and sliced

2 tablespoons chopped sweet onion

Pecan halves, toasted (optional)

For Vinaigrette: In a screw-top jar combine pear nectar, salad oil, raspberry vinegar, Dijon-style mustard, toasted sesame oil, basil, and pepper. Cover and shake well.

To Prepare Poultry: Place chicken in a plastic bag set into a shallow bowl. Reserve half of the vinaigrette for dressing. Pour remaining vinaigrette over chicken in bag. Seal bag and turn chicken to coat well. Marinate at room temperature for 15 minutes. Drain chicken, reserving marinade.

To Cook by Direct Grill Method: Place chicken and asparagus on the rack of an uncovered grill. Grill directly over medium coals for 12 to 15 minutes or until chicken and asparagus are tender and chicken is no longer pink, turning and brushing once with marinade halfway through grilling. Discard remaining marinade.

To Serve: Divide greens between 2 dinner plates. Slice chicken into strips; arrange on greens. Top with asparagus, strawberries, pear, and onion. Drizzle with dressing. If desired, sprinkle with pecans. Makes 2 servings.

Nutrition Facts per serving: 379 cal., 20 g total fat (3 g sat. fat), 59 mg chol., 131 mg sodium, 28 g carbo., 25 g pro.

orange-glazed chicken

Soy sauce and five-spice powder add a touch of the Orient to this honey-and-orange sauced chicken dish.

1/3 cup frozen orange juice concentrate, thawed

1/4 cup honey

1/4 cup soy sauce

1 teaspoon five-spice powder

1/2 teaspoon garlic powder

2 pounds meaty chicken pieces (breasts, thighs, and drumsticks)

1 small orange

For Glaze: In a small mixing bowl combine orange juice, honey, soy sauce, five-spice powder, and garlic powder. Set aside.

To Prepare Poultry: If desired, remove skin from the chicken.

To Cook by Indirect Grill Method: In a covered grill arrange preheated coals around a drip pan. Test for medium heat above the pan. Place chicken, bone side down, on the grill rack over the drip pan. Cover and grill for 50 to 60 minutes or until chicken is tender and no longer pink, brushing occasionally with glaze the last 10 minutes of grilling.

To Cook by Direct Grill Method: Place chicken, bone side up, on the grill rack of an uncovered grill. Grill directly over medium coals for 35 to 45 minutes or until chicken is tender and no longer pink, turning once halfway through grilling time and brushing occasionally with glaze the last 10 minutes of grilling.

To Serve: Cut the orange into thin slices. Garnish chicken with orange slices. Makes 4 servings.

Nutrition Facts per serving: 387 cal., 13 g total fat (3 g sat. fat), 104 mg chol., 1,123 mg sodium, 33 g carbo., 35 g pro.

tips from the kitchen

testing the coals
Judging the temperature of coals without a thermometer is a guess, but it can be an educated one. Many chefs determine the coal temperature by how long they can hold their hand above the coals at the cooking level. A medium fire, which most of the recipes in this book call for, equates to a hand count of 4 seconds and a temperature reading of 350° to 375°. At this point, the coals should glow through a layer of gray ash.

curried chicken

A spicy sweet sauce perks up grilled chicken pieces.

3 tablespoons honey

2 tablespoons dry white wine or white wine vinegar

2 teaspoons curry powder

1/2 teaspoon garlic salt

1/4 teaspoon paprika

Dash ground red pepper

2 pounds meaty chicken pieces (breasts, thighs, and drumsticks)

For Sauce: In a small mixing bowl combine honey, wine, curry powder, garlic salt, paprika, and red pepper. Set aside.

To Prepare Poultry: If desired, remove skin from the chicken.

To Cook by Indirect Grill Method: In a covered grill arrange preheated coals around a drip pan. Test for medium heat above the pan. Place chicken, bone side down, on the grill rack over the drip pan. Cover and grill for 50 to 60 minutes or until chicken is tender and no longer pink, brushing frequently with sauce the last 10 minutes of grilling.

To Cook by Direct Grill Method: Place chicken, bone side up, on the grill rack of an uncovered grill. Grill directly over medium coals for 35 to 45 minutes or until chicken is tender and no longer pink, turning once halfway through grilling time and brushing frequently with sauce the last 10 minutes of grilling. Makes 4 servings.

Nutrition Facts per serving: 308 cal., 13 g total fat (3 g sat. fat), 104 mg chol., 307 mg sodium, 14 g carbo., 33 g pro.

chicken pinwheels

Welcome spring with these succulent chicken breasts. Serve them with steamed asparagus and pasta tossed with butter and Parmesan cheese.

4 skinless, boneless chicken breast halves (about 1 pound total)

2 to 3 ounces thinly sliced prosciutto or very thinly sliced ham

2 tablespoons margarine or butter, melted

1 tablespoon lemon juice

1/2 teaspoon dried thyme, crushed

1/4 teaspoon garlic powder

To Prepare Poultry: Cut chicken into ½-inch-wide strips. Cut prosciutto into ½-inch-wide strips. Divide the chicken and prosciutto strips into 4 portions. Place a strip of prosciutto on each strip of chicken. For each serving, form one strip into a pinwheel with prosciutto inside. Add remaining strips, one at a time, forming a large pinwheel with prosciutto inside; secure with wooden toothpicks. Repeat with other strips to form 4 pinwheels total.

For Sauce: In a small mixing bowl stir together margarine, lemon juice, thyme, and garlic powder.

To Cook by Indirect Grill Method: Brush pinwheels with sauce. In a covered grill arrange preheated coals around a drip pan. Test for medium heat above the pan. Place pinwheels on the grill rack over the drip pan. Cover and grill for 11 to 13 minutes or until chicken is tender and no longer pink, turning once and brushing with sauce halfway through grilling time.

To Cook by Direct Grill Method: Brush pinwheels with sauce. Place pinwheels on the grill rack of an uncovered grill. Grill directly over medium coals about 10 minutes or until chicken is tender and no longer pink, turning once and brushing with sauce halfway through grilling time. Makes 4 servings.

Nutrition Facts per serving: 218 cal., 12 g total fat (2 g sat. fat), 59 mg chol., 371 mg sodium, 0 g carbo., 25 g pro.

honey-soy grilled chicken

Marinate 24 hours for maximum flavor in this honey-soy dish.

1/4 cup water

1/4 cup soy sauce

1/4 cup dry sherry

1 green onion, sliced

2 cloves garlic, minced

1/2 teaspoon five-spice powder

1 3- to 4-pound broiler-fryer chicken

1 tablespoon cooking oil

1 tablespoon honey

For Marinade: In a small bowl combine water, soy sauce, sherry, green onion, garlic, and five-spice powder.

To Prepare Poultry: Remove the neck and giblets from chicken. Skewer the neck skin to the back. Twist wing tips under back. Tie legs to tail with 100-percent-cotton string. Place chicken in a plastic bag set in a deep bowl. Pour marinade over chicken in bag. Seal bag and turn chicken to coat well. Marinate in the refrigerator for 6 to 24 hours, turning bag occasionally. Drain chicken, discarding marinade. Brush chicken with oil.

To Cook by Indirect Grill Method. In a covered grill arrange preheated coals around a drip pan. Test for medium heat above the pan. Place chicken, breast side up, on grill rack over drip pan. Cover and grill for 1¼ to

1¾ hours or until drumsticks move easily (180°), brushing often with the honey the last 10 minutes of grilling. Remove chicken from grill.

To Serve: Cover with foil; let stand for 10 minutes before carving. Makes 6 to 8 servings.

Nutrition Facts per serving: 251 cal., 14 g total fat (4 g sat. fat), 79 mg chol., 245 mg sodium, 3 g carbo., 25 g pro.

cranberry-glazed turkey drumsticks

We suggest half of a turkey drumstick per serving, but you may want to serve whole ones to those who crave dark meat and possess hearty appetites.

1   16-ounce can whole cranberry sauce

¹/₂ cup apricot preserves

2   tablespoons lemon juice

2   turkey drumsticks (1 to 1¹/₂ pounds) each or 8 chicken drumsticks (about 1¹/₂ pounds total)

1   tablespoon vegetable oil

For Sauce: In a small saucepan combine cranberry sauce, apricot preserves, and lemon juice. Cook and stir until bubbly. Remove from heat; set aside.

To Prepare Poultry: Remove skin from turkey or chicken drumsticks. Brush with oil.

To Cook by Indirect Grill Method: In a covered grill arrange preheated coals around a drip pan. Test for medium heat above the pan. Place turkey on a rack in a pan on the grill rack. (Place chicken on the grill rack above a drip pan.) Cover and grill for 1¾ to 2 hours for turkey or 50 to 60 minutes for chicken or until poultry is tender and no longer pink, brushing frequently with sauce the last 10 minutes of grilling.

To Serve: Heat remaining sauce. Cut the meat from the turkey drumsticks. Serve turkey or chicken with sauce. Makes 4 servings.

Nutrition Facts per serving: 543 cal., 12 g total fat (4 g sat. fat), 107 mg chol., 133 mg sodium, 73 g carbo., 35 g pro.

tips from the kitchen

don't get burned Taking a few precautions when cooking poultry will ensure a dish that is wholesome and safe. 1) Don't thaw poultry on the countertop or in the sink because bacteria reproduces faster at room temperature. 2) Wash your hands, utensils, cutting boards, and work surfaces with hot water after handling poultry to prevent spreading bacteria to other foods. 3) Use separate dishes for raw and cooked poultry.

turkey with ginger salsa

Stirring a little of the ginger marinade into fresh tomato salsa creates a flavorful poultry relish.

- ¹/₄ cup vinegar
- 2 tablespoons dry sherry
- 2 tablespoons soy sauce
- 1 tablespoon grated fresh ginger
- 1 clove garlic, minced
- 1 teaspoon crushed red pepper
- 4 turkey breast tenderloin steaks (about 1 pound total)
- 1 medium tomato, peeled, seeded, and chopped
- 1 green onion, sliced (2 tablespoons)
- ¹/₄ cup chopped sweet green pepper
- 1 tablespoon snipped fresh cilantro
- 4 6-inch flour tortillas

For Marinade: In a small mixing bowl combine vinegar, sherry, soy sauce, ginger, garlic, and red pepper. Reserve 2 tablespoons of the marinade for salsa.

To Prepare Poultry: Place turkey in a plastic bag set into a deep bowl. Pour marinade over turkey in bag. Seal bag and turn turkey to coat well. Marinate in the refrigerator for 6 to 24 hours, turning bag occasionally. Remove turkey from bag, reserving marinade.

For Salsa: In a small mixing bowl combine tomato, green onion, sweet green pepper, cilantro, and the 2 tablespoons reserved marinade. (Do not use the mixture in which turkey was marinated.) Cover and chill salsa until serving time.

To Cook by Indirect Grill Method: In a covered grill arrange preheated coals around a drip pan. Test for medium heat above the pan. Place turkey on the grill rack over the drip pan. Cover and grill for 15 to 18 minutes or until turkey is tender and no longer pink, brushing with marinade after 10 minutes. Discard remaining marinade.

To Cook by Direct Grill Method: Place turkey on the grill rack of an uncovered grill. Grill directly over medium coals for 12 to 15 minutes or until turkey is tender and no longer pink, turning once and brushing with reserved marinade halfway through grilling time. Discard remaining marinade.

To Serve: Place tortillas in a single layer on the grill rack for 1 minute. Serve turkey with warmed tortillas and chilled salsa. Makes 4 servings.

Nutrition Facts per serving: 208 cal., 4 g total fat (1 g sat. fat), 50 mg chol., 564 mg sodium, 18 g carbo., 24 g pro.

double-glazed turkey breasts

Two recipes in one! Each turkey breast half is brushed with a different glaze.

- **4** cups hickory wood chips or mesquite wood chips (optional)
- **¹/₃** cup orange marmalade
- **1** tablespoon hoisin sauce
- **¹/₄** teaspoon five-spice powder
- **¹/₄** teaspoon garlic powder
- **¹/₄** cup honey
- **1** tablespoon Dijon-style mustard
- **1** tablespoon white wine Worcestershire sauce
- **1** tablespoon margarine or butter, melted
- **2** 2- to 2¹/₂-pound turkey breast halves
- **1** tablespoon cooking oil

To Prepare Wood Chips: If using, at least 1 hour before grilling, soak wood chips in enough water to cover. Drain chips before using.

For Five-Spice Glaze: In a small mixing bowl stir together orange marmalade, hoisin sauce, five-spice powder, and garlic powder. Set aside.

For Honey-Mustard Glaze: In a small mixing bowl stir together honey, Dijon-style mustard, Worcestershire sauce, and margarine. Set aside.

To Prepare Turkey: Remove bone from turkey breasts. Brush turkey with oil. Insert a meat thermometer into the center of one of the turkey breasts.

To Cook by Indirect Grill Method: In a covered grill arrange preheated coals around a drip pan. Test for medium heat above the pan. If using, sprinkle 1 cup of the drained wood chips onto the preheated coals. Place the turkey breasts, side by side, on a rack in a roasting pan on the grill rack. Cover and grill for 1½ to 2 hours or until thermometer registers 170°, brushing one breast half with Five-Spice Glaze and the other breast half with Honey-Mustard Glaze several times the last 15 minutes of grilling. Add additional coals and drained wood chips, if using, every 20 to 30 minutes or as necessary to maintain medium heat.

To Serve: Heat any of the remaining glazes. Pass the glazes with the sliced turkey. Makes 10 servings.

Nutrition Facts per serving: *171 cal., 5 g total fat (1 g sat. fat), 40 mg chol., 150 mg sodium, 15 g carbo., 16 g pro.*

pineapple-rum turkey kabobs

When you eat this rum-and-lemongrass kabob, you won't know whether you're in the Caribbean or the South Seas, but you'll like it just the same.

1/3 cup unsweetened pineapple juice

3 tablespoons rum or unsweetened pineapple juice

1 tablespoon brown sugar

1 tablespoon finely chopped lemongrass or 2 teaspoons finely shredded lemon peel

1 tablespoon olive oil

12 ounces turkey breast tenderloin steaks, cut 1/2 inch thick, or boneless turkey breast

1 medium red onion, cut into thin wedges

3 plums or 2 nectarines, pitted and cut into thick slices

2 cups fresh or canned pineapple chunks

Hot cooked rice (optional)

Thinly sliced sugar snap peas (optional)

For Marinade: In a small mixing bowl combine the 1/3 cup pineapple juice, the rum or 3 tablespoons pineapple juice, brown sugar, lemongrass or lemon peel, and olive oil. Set aside.

To Prepare Poultry: Cut turkey into 1-inch cubes. Place turkey in a plastic bag set in a shallow bowl. Pour marinade over turkey in bag. Seal bag and turn turkey to coat well. Marinate in the refrigerator for 4 to 24 hours, turning the bag occasionally. Drain turkey, reserving the marinade.

In a small saucepan bring marinade to boiling. Boil gently for 1 minute. Remove from heat. On four 12-inch metal skewers, alternately thread turkey and onion, leaving about a 1/4-inch space between pieces. Alternately thread the plums and the pineapple onto 4 more skewers.

To Cook by Direct Grill Method: Place turkey kabobs on the rack of an uncovered grill. Grill directly over medium coals for 12 to 14 minutes or until turkey and onion are tender and turkey is no longer pink, turning once and brushing occasionally with marinade during the last half of grilling. Add fruit kabobs for the last 5 minutes of grilling to heat through, turning once and brushing occasionally with marinade.

To Serve: If desired, toss hot cooked rice with snap peas. Serve turkey, onion, and fruit with rice. Makes 4 servings.

Nutrition Facts per serving: 235 cal., 6 g total fat (1 g sat. fat), 37 mg chol., 37 mg sodium, 24 g carbo., 17 g pro.

spicy turkey tenderloins

These turkey tenderloins need only 20 minutes to marinate. If desired, let them soak an hour for maximum flavor.

   2 turkey breast tenderloins

   1 teaspoon finely shredded
      orange peel

 1/4 cup orange juice

   2 tablespoons olive oil or cooking oil

   1 teaspoon ground cumin

   1 teaspoon dried thyme, crushed

   1 medium onion, chopped (1/2 cup)

 1/2 teaspoon salt

 1/4 teaspoon black pepper

 1/4 teaspoon crushed red pepper

To Prepare Turkey: Place turkey tenderloins in a shallow, nonmetal dish.

For Marinade: In small bowl combine orange peel, orange juice, olive or cooking oil, cumin, thyme, onion, salt, black pepper, and crushed red pepper. Pour

marinade over turkey. Cover and let stand 20 minutes. Drain turkey, reserving the marinade.

To Cook by Direct Grill Method: Grill turkey on the rack of an uncovered grill directly over medium coals for 12 to 15 minutes or until turkey is tender and no longer pink, turning once halfway through the grilling and brushing with the marinade during the first 6 minutes of grilling. Makes 4 servings.

Nutrition Facts per serving: 182 cal., 9 g total fat (2 g sat. fat), 50 mg chol., 315 mg sodium, 2 g carbo., 22 g pro.

teriyaki turkey patties

Chopped water chestnuts add just the right amount of crunch to these extraordinary orange-glazed turkey burgers.

- **1** beaten egg
- **1/2** cup soft bread crumbs
- **1/4** cup chopped water chestnuts
- **2** tablespoons chopped onion
- **1** tablespoon teriyaki sauce
- **1** pound ground raw turkey
- **1/4** cup orange marmalade
- **1** tablespoon teriyaki sauce
- **1/2** teaspoon sesame seed

To Prepare Poultry Mixture: In a medium mixing bowl combine egg, bread crumbs, water chestnuts, onion, and 1 tablespoon teriyaki sauce. Add ground turkey and mix well. Shape the mixture into four ¾-inch-thick patties. (Mixture will be soft.)

To Cook by Indirect Grill Method: In a covered grill arrange preheated coals around a drip pan. Test for medium heat above the pan. Place patties on the grill rack over the drip pan. Cover and grill for 20 to 24 minutes or until juices run clear, turning once halfway through grilling time.

To Cook by Direct Grill Method: Grill patties on the grill rack of an uncovered grill directly over medium coals for 14 to 18 minutes or until done (165°), turning once halfway through grilling time.

For Sauce: In a small saucepan combine orange marmalade, 1 tablespoon teriyaki sauce, and the sesame seed. Cook over low heat until marmalade melts, stirring occasionally.

To Serve: Spoon sauce over cooked patties. Makes 4 servings.

Nutrition Facts per serving: 240 cal., 10 g total fat (3 g sat. fat), 95 mg chol., 400 mg sodium, 19 g carbo., 18 g pro.

cider-glazed turkey with sweet potatoes

Candied sweet potatoes and apples cook along side the turkey thighs in this traditional combination that can be served at Thanksgiving or anytime of year.

$^1/_2$ cup apple cider or apple juice

2 tablespoons apple jelly

1 teaspoon cornstarch

$^1/_4$ teaspoon ground nutmeg

12 ounces sweet potatoes (about 2 medium), peeled and cut into $^1/_2$-inch-thick slices

2 medium apples, cut in wedges

2 small turkey thighs (2 pounds total)

For Sauce: In a small saucepan stir together apple cider, apple jelly, cornstarch, and nutmeg. Cook and stir until thickened and bubbly. Cook and stir for 2 minutes more. Remove from heat; set aside.

To Prepare Sweet Potatoes: Toss together sweet potatoes and apples. Tear off a 36×18-inch piece of heavy foil. Fold in half to make a double thickness of foil that measures 18×18 inches. Place sweet potato mixture in the center of the foil. Drizzle with half of the sauce. Bring up two opposite edges of foil and seal with a double fold. Then fold remaining ends to completely encase the packet, leaving space for steam to build. Refrigerate the packet until ready to grill.

To Prepare Poultry: Remove skin from turkey thighs, if desired. Insert meat thermometer into the center of one of the turkey thighs, not touching bone.

To Cook by Indirect Grill Method: In a covered grill arrange preheated coals around a drip pan. Test for medium heat above the pan. Place turkey thighs, bone side down, on rack in a roasting pan on the grill rack. Cover and grill for 1¼ to 1¾ hours or until meat thermometer inserted registers 180°, brushing frequently with sauce the last 10 minutes of grilling. Place the foil packet containing the sweet potatoes beside the pan with turkey thighs on the grill rack, not over coals. Grill foil packet the last 30 to 40 minutes of grilling.

To Serve: Cut the turkey meat from the bones. Serve with sweet potatoes. Makes 4 servings.

Nutrition Facts per serving: 354 cal., 7 g total fat (2 g sat. fat), 83 mg chol., 105 mg sodium, 37 g carbo., 35 g pro.

caesar turkey and penne salad

Traditional Caesar salad gets a new spin with the addition of pasta.

6 ounces packaged dried gemelli or penne pasta

4 turkey breast tenderloin steaks, cut $^1/_2$ inch thick (about 1 pound total)

$^3/_4$ cup bottled Caesar salad dressing

6 cups torn romaine lettuce

12 cherry tomatoes, halved

$^1/_4$ cup finely shredded Parmesan cheese

Black pepper (optional)

Cook pasta according to package directions; drain.

To Cook by Direct Grill Method: Place turkey on the grill rack of an uncovered grill. Grill directly over medium coals for 12 to 15 minutes or until tender and no longer pink, turning and brushing once with ¼ cup of the salad dressing halfway through grilling. Transfer turkey to a cutting board; cool slightly.

To Serve: In a large salad bowl combine cooked pasta, romaine, and tomatoes. Add the remaining salad dressing; toss gently to coat. Slice turkey diagonally across the grain and arrange on greens mixture. Sprinkle with Parmesan cheese and, if desired, pepper. Makes 4 servings.

Nutrition Facts per serving: 538 cal., 26 g total fat (1 g sat. fat), 55 mg chol., 138 mg sodium, 41 g carbo., 32 g pro.

mustard-glazed turkey drumsticks

Stir together mustard and vinegar for an almost-instant glaze.

$^1/_4$ cup coarse-grain brown mustard, hot-style mustard, horseradish mustard, or sweet-hot mustard

1 tablespoon vinegar

2 turkey drumsticks (1 to 1$^1/_2$ pounds each)

1 to 2 tablespoons cooking oil

For Glaze: In a small mixing bowl stir together mustard and vinegar. Set aside.

Prepare Turkey: Remove skin from turkey drumsticks. Brush drumsticks with oil.

To Cook by Indirect Grill Method: In a covered grill arrange preheated coals for indirect cooking. Test for medium heat where turkey will cook. Place turkey on a rack in a roasting pan on the grill rack. Cover and grill for 1 to 1¼ hours or until turkey is tender and no longer pink, turning once and brushing occasionally with glaze after 30 minutes.

To Serve: Cut the meat from the drumsticks. Makes 4 servings.

Nutrition Facts per serving: 213 cal., 13 g total fat (3 g sat. fat), 68 mg chol., 262 mg sodium, 1 g carbo., 22 g pro.

savory grilled turkey with summer squash

Stuffing the bird with garlic produces a subtle trace of flavor in every bite.

4 cups hickory or other wood chips (optional)

Summer Squash Casserole (recipe, page 77)

1 6- to 8-pound fresh turkey or frozen turkey, thawed

4 cloves elephant garlic, halved, or 8 to 10 regular garlic cloves (optional)

Cooking oil

To Prepare Wood Chips: If using, at least 1 hour before grilling, soak wood chips in enough water to cover. Drain the chips before using.

To Prepare Accompaniment: Prepare Summer Squash Casserole (recipe, page 77). Refrigerate the packet until ready to grill.

To Prepare Turkey: Remove the neck and giblets from turkey. Skewer the neck skin to the back. If desired, place garlic in the body cavity. Tuck drumsticks under the band of skin across the tail. Twist wing tips under the back. Insert a meat thermometer into the center of the inside thigh muscle, not touching the bone.

To Cook by Indirect Grill Method: In a covered grill arrange preheated coals for indirect cooking. Test for medium heat where turkey will cook. If using, sprinkle 1 cup of the drained wood chips onto the preheated coals. Place the turkey, breast side up, on a rack in a roasting pan on the grill rack. Brush the turkey with cooking oil. Cover and grill for 1¾ to 2¼ hours or until meat thermometer registers 180°, brushing occasionally with cooking oil. Add additional coals and drained wood chips, if using, every 20 to 30 minutes or as necessary to maintain medium heat. Place the foil packet of Summer Squash Casserole beside the turkey on the grill rack. Grill foil packet directly over medium-high coals the last 20 minutes of grilling.

To Serve: Remove turkey from the grill. Let turkey stand, covered, for 15 minutes before carving. Serve with Summer Squash Casserole. Makes 8 servings.

Nutrition Facts per serving: 275 cal., 10 g total fat (3 g sat. fat), 108 mg chol., 101 mg sodium, 1 g carbo., 42 g pro.

zippy cornish game hens

Horseradish, pepper, and allspice give these marinated game hens their "zip."

½ cup water

½ of a 5-ounce jar prepared horseradish (¼ cup)

2 tablespoons lemon juice

1 teaspoon ground black pepper

½ teaspoon ground allspice

2 1¼- to 1½-pound Cornish game hens, halved lengthwise (thawed, if frozen)

¼ cup margarine or butter, melted

1 teaspoon finely shredded lemon peel

Prepared horseradish (optional)

For Marinade: In a small mixing bowl combine water, the ¼ cup horseradish, the lemon juice, pepper, and allspice. Set aside.

To Prepare Cornish Hens: If desired, remove skin from hens. Place hens in a plastic bag set into a deep bowl.

Pour marinade over hens in bag. Seal bag and turn hens to coat well. Marinate in the refrigerator for 6 to 24 hours, turning bag occasionally. Remove hens from bag; discard the marinade.

For Sauce: In a small saucepan melt margarine or butter. Stir in lemon peel.

To Cook by Indirect Grill Method: In a covered grill arrange preheated coals around a drip pan. Test for medium heat above the pan. Place hens, bone side down, on a rack in a roasting pan on the grill rack. Cover and grill about 1 hour or until meat is tender and no longer pink (180°), brushing occasionally with sauce.

To Serve: If desired, serve with additional horseradish. Makes 4 servings.

Nutrition Facts per serving: 250 cal., 21 g total fat (4 g sat. fat), 50 mg chol., 259 mg sodium, 1 g carbo., 15 g pro.

chicken mole sandwich

It's the mole that makes this sandwich a zinger. Would you believe a sauce of chocolate and Mexican chile peppers could taste this good?

1/4 cup chopped onion

3 cloves garlic minced

1 tablespoon cooking oil

1/2 cup water

3 dried chile peppers (New Mexico or pasilla), seeded and coarsely chopped

3 tablespoons chopped Mexican-style sweet chocolate or semisweet chocolate (1 1/2 ounces)

4 medium skinless, boneless chicken breast halves (about 1 pound total)

Salt (optional)

1 small avocado, seeded, peeled, and mashed

2 tablespoons light mayonnaise dressing

1/4 teaspoon ground red pepper (optional)

1/8 teaspoon salt

4 hard rolls (about 6 inches in diameter), split and toasted

Tomato slices

Baby romaine or other lettuce leaves

For Mole: In a large skillet cook onion and garlic in hot oil over medium-high heat until onion is tender. Add water and dried chile peppers. Reduce heat to medium; stir in chocolate. Cook and stir for 3 to 5 minutes or until thickened and bubbly. Cool slightly. Transfer mixture to a food processor bowl or blender container. Cover and process or blend until a smooth paste forms. Reserve 1 to 2 tablespoons of the mole.

To Prepare Poultry: If desired, sprinkle chicken with salt. Using a sharp knife, cut a slit horizontally two-thirds of the way through each chicken piece. Spread meat open; fill with remaining mole. Fold closed. Rub the outside of the chicken with the reserved mole.

To Cook by Direct Grill Method: Place chicken on the grill rack of an uncovered grill. Grill directly over medium coals for 12 to 15 minutes or until tender and no longer pink, turning once halfway through grilling. Cover and chill in the refrigerator for 30 minutes.

For Sauce: In a small bowl stir together avocado, mayonnaise dressing, ground red pepper (if desired), and the 1/8 teaspoon salt.

To Serve: Cut chicken into 1/4- to 1/2-inch slices. Spread sauce on split rolls; layer with tomato, chicken, and romaine. Makes 4 servings.

Nutrition Facts per serving: 496 cal., 22 g total fat (5 g sat. fat), 59 mg chol., 542 mg sodium, 45 g carbo., 30 g pro.

beef, pork, & lamb

Jalapeño Beef Kabobs
(recipe, page 38)

chimichanga-style beef bundles

Grilling makes the tortilla shells crisp and crunchy. Serve with Spanish rice and refried beans.

6 10-inch flour tortillas

1 pound lean ground beef

1/2 cup chopped onion (1 medium)

1 clove garlic, minced

1 large tomato, peeled, seeded, and chopped

1 4-ounce can diced green chile peppers, drained

1/4 teaspoon salt

1/4 teaspoon ground cumin

Several dashes bottled hot pepper sauce

2 cups shredded Monterey Jack cheese (8 ounces)

1 6-ounce container frozen avocado dip, thawed, or 1 cup salsa

Fresh cilantro (optional)

For Tortillas: Wrap the tortillas in foil and heat in a 350° oven for 10 minutes to soften.

To Prepare Meat Mixture: Meanwhile, in a large skillet cook beef, onion, and garlic until meat is brown and onion is tender. Drain off fat. Stir in tomato, chile peppers, salt, cumin, and hot pepper sauce. Remove one tortilla at a time from foil packet and spoon about ½ cup of the meat mixture just below the center of the tortilla. Sprinkle with ⅓ cup of the cheese. Fold bottom edge of tortilla up and over filling, just until mixture is covered. Fold opposite sides of tortilla in, just until they meet. Roll filled section over onto opposite edge of tortilla. If necessary, secure with wooden toothpicks. Repeat with remaining tortillas, meat, and cheese.

To Cook by Indirect Grill Method: In a covered grill arrange preheated coals around a drip pan. Test for medium-low heat above the pan. Place packets, seam side down, on the grill rack over the drip pan. Cover and grill for 20 to 25 minutes or until heated through.

To Cook by Direct Grill Method: Place packets, seam side down, on the grill rack of an uncovered grill directly over medium-low coals for 15 to 20 minutes or until heated through, turning once halfway through grilling time.

To Serve: Top each packet with avocado dip or salsa. If desired, garnish with sprigs of cilantro. Makes 6 servings.

Nutrition Facts per serving: 431 cal., 22 g total fat (10 g sat. fat), 81 mg chol., 411 mg sodium, 30 g carbo., 27 g pro.

lemon-dill marinated flank steak

A summer-style recipe—a marinade that's easy to put together, and a meat that's quick to grill.

2 green onions, sliced (¹/₄ cup)

¹/₄ cup water

¹/₄ cup dry red wine

¹/₄ cup soy sauce

3 tablespoons lemon juice

2 tablespoons cooking oil

1 tablespoon snipped fresh dill or
   1 teaspoon dried dillweed

1 tablespoon Worcestershire sauce

2 cloves garlic, minced

¹/₂ teaspoon celery seed

¹/₂ teaspoon black pepper

1 1- to 1¹/₂-pound beef flank steak,
   cut about ³/₄ inch thick

tips from the kitchen

make it tender *Flank steak is a great steak for grilling. But, unless you tenderize it by marinating or tenderizing, you're in for some real tug-of-war when you bite into it. Once marinated, flank steak is perfect for both broiling and grilling. To serve, use a sharp knife to cut across the grain into very thin slices.*

For Marinade: In a medium mixing bowl combine green onions, water, wine, soy sauce, lemon juice, cooking oil, dill, Worcestershire sauce, garlic, celery seed, and pepper.

To Prepare Meat: Score meat by making shallow cuts at 1-inch intervals diagonally across the steak in a diamond pattern. Repeat scoring on the second side. Place steak in a plastic bag set into a shallow dish. Pour marinade over steak in bag. Seal bag and turn steak to coat well. Marinate in the refrigerator for 6 to 24 hours, turning bag occasionally. Remove steak from bag, reserving the marinade.

To Cook by Indirect Grill Method: In a covered grill arrange preheated coals around a drip pan. Test for medium heat above the pan. Place steak on the grill rack over the drip pan. Cover and grill for 18 to 22 minutes for medium doneness (160°), turning once and brushing with reserved marinade halfway through grilling time. Discard remaining marinade.

To Cook by Direct Grill Method: Grill steak on the grill rack of an uncovered grill directly over medium coals for 12 to 14 minutes for medium doneness (160°), turning once and brushing with reserved marinade halfway through grilling time. Discard remaining marinade.

To Serve: Slice the meat diagonally across the grain into very thin slices. Makes 4 servings.

Nutrition Facts per serving: 201 cal., 10 g total fat (3 g sat. fat), 53 mg chol., 206 mg sodium, 1 g carbo., 22 g pro.

mushroom-horseradish-stuffed steaks

Serve these flavorful top loin steaks with Caramelized Onion and Cheese Bites (see recipe, page 74). Be sure to set out additional horseradish on the table for those who like added zing.

1½ cups sliced fresh mushrooms

1 medium onion, chopped (½ cup)

2 cloves garlic, minced

1 tablespoon margarine or butter

2 tablespoons prepared horseradish

¼ teaspoon salt

⅛ teaspoon black pepper

4 10-ounce beef top loin steaks, cut 1 inch thick

2 tablespoons margarine or butter, melted

1 tablespoon Worcestershire sauce

For Stuffing: In a medium saucepan cook mushrooms, onion, and garlic in the 1 tablespoon margarine or butter until tender. Stir in horseradish, salt, and pepper.

To Prepare Meat: Trim fat from meat. Cut a pocket in each steak by cutting from the fat side almost to, but not through, other side. Spoon the stuffing into the steak pockets. Fasten pockets with wooden toothpicks.

For Sauce: In a small mixing bowl combine the 2 tablespoons margarine or butter and the Worcestershire sauce.

To Cook by Indirect Grill Method: In a covered grill arrange preheated coals around a drip pan. Test for medium heat above the pan. Place meat on the grill rack over the drip pan. Cover and grill for 20 to 24 minutes for medium doneness (160°), turning once and brushing with sauce the last 10 minutes of grilling.

To Cook by Direct Grill Method: Grill steaks on the grill rack of an uncovered grill directly over medium coals for 12 to 15 minutes for medium doneness (160°), turning once and brushing with sauce. Makes 4 servings.

Nutrition Facts per serving: 487 cal., 26 g total fat (8 g sat. fat), 150 mg chol., 486 mg sodium, 5 g carbo., 56 g pro.

steaks with blue cheese butter

This recipe makes more blue cheese butter than you'll need for the steak. Cover and chill the extra butter and serve it over vegetables at your next meal. (Recipe also pictured on front cover.)

$^1/_2$ cup butter or margarine, softened

$^1/_2$ cup crumbled blue cheese (2 ounces)

1   tablespoon snipped fresh parsley

1   tablespoon snipped fresh basil or
1 teaspoon dried basil, crushed

1   clove garlic, minced

2   beef porterhouse or T-bone steaks,
cut 1 to 1$^1/_4$ inches thick

For Butter: In a small mixing bowl stir together butter or margarine, blue cheese, parsley, basil, and garlic. Set aside.

To Prepare Meat: Trim fat from steaks.

To Cook by Direct Grill Method: Place steaks on the grill rack of an uncovered grill. Grill directly over medium coals for 12 to 18 minutes for medium doneness (160°), turning once halfway through grilling.

To Serve: Cut steaks into serving-size pieces. Top each piece with a generous 1 tablespoon of the butter mixture. Cover and chill the remaining butter in the refrigerator for another time. (Butter can be tossed with hot cooked vegetables.) Makes 4 servings.

Nutrition Facts per serving: 458 cal., 28 g total fat (13 g sat. fat), 161 mg chol., 270 mg sodium, 0 g carbo., 49 g pro.

barbecued beef ribs

Serve coleslaw and baked beans alongside these all-American beef ribs. Finish the meal with big bowls of your favorite flavor of ice cream.

3 to 4 pounds beef chuck short ribs with bone or 2 to 2¹/₂ pounds without bone

1 8-ounce can tomato sauce

¹/₄ cup water

2 tablespoons brown sugar

2 tablespoons vinegar or lemon juice

1 tablespoon Worcestershire sauce

1 tablespoon finely chopped onion

1 teaspoon crushed red pepper

To Precook Ribs: Trim fat from meat. Cut ribs into serving-size pieces. Place ribs in a Dutch oven. Add enough water to cover ribs. Bring to boiling; reduce heat. Cover and simmer about 2 hours or until meat is tender. Drain ribs.

For Sauce: Meanwhile, in a small saucepan combine tomato sauce, water, brown sugar, vinegar, Worcestershire sauce, onion, and red pepper. Bring to boiling; reduce heat. Simmer, uncovered, for 10 minutes, stirring once or twice. Remove from heat.

To Cook by Indirect Grill Method: In a covered grill arrange preheated coals around a drip pan. Test for medium heat above the pan. Place precooked ribs on the grill rack over the drip pan. Brush with the sauce. Cover and grill for 15 minutes, brushing occasionally with the sauce. Makes 4 servings.

Nutrition Facts per serving: 510 cal., 19 g total fat (8 g sat. fat), 97 mg chol., 338 mg sodium, 8 g carbo., 33 g pro.

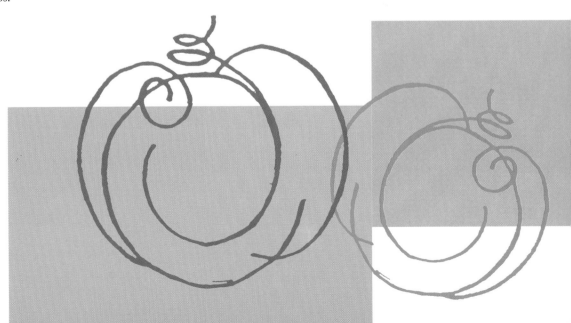

herbed chuck roast

Lemon and fresh rosemary flavor this beef chuck pot roast. Serve with Herbed Sourdough Bread (see recipe, page 80) and cooked carrots.

1 cup vinegar

1 cup water

2 medium onions, sliced

1/2 lemon, sliced

2 tablespoons snipped fresh rosemary or 2 teaspoons dried rosemary, crushed

1 teaspoon salt

1 teaspoon black pepper

1 3- to 4-pound beef chuck pot roast, cut 2 inches thick

tips from the kitchen

timing is everything Cooking times given in a recipe are only approximations because of the many variables affecting the process—wind, outside temperature, rain, thickness and shape of the meat, doneness preference, distance between the fire and the food, and the food's temperature when placed on the grill. Extra charcoal briquettes, a grill cover, and a longer cooking time are often required on cold or windy days.

For Marinade: In a medium mixing bowl combine vinegar, water, onions, lemon, rosemary, salt, and the pepper.

To Prepare Meat: Trim fat from meat. Place meat in a plastic bag set into a deep bowl. Pour marinade over meat in bag. Seal bag and turn meat to coat well. Marinate in the refrigerator for 6 to 24 hours, turning bag occasionally. Remove meat from bag; discard the marinade.

To Cook by Indirect Grill Method: In a covered grill arrange preheated coals around a drip pan. Test for medium heat above the the pan. Place meat on a rack in a roasting pan on the grill rack. Cover and grill for 1 hour 25 minutes for medium doneness (160°). Makes 4 servings.

Nutrition Facts per serving: 228 cal., 10 g total fat (4 g sat. fat), 99 mg chol., 118 mg sodium, 1 g carbo., 32 g pro.

jalapeño beef kabobs

Firecracker-hot but as sweet-as-pie, jalapeño pepper jelly adds zing to these kabobs. Look for it with other jams and jellies at the supermarket. (Recipe pictured on pages 30-31.)

1   10-ounce jar jalapeño pepper jelly

2   tablespoons lime juice

1   clove garlic, minced

4   small purple or white boiling onions

4   baby pattypan squash, halved
    crosswise

1   pound boneless beef sirloin steak, cut
    1 inch thick

4   fresh tomatillos, husked and cut into
    quarters

$^1/_2$ of a medium red or green sweet
    pepper, cut into 1-inch squares

    Hot cooked polenta (optional)

For Glaze: In a small saucepan combine the jalapeño jelly, lime juice, and garlic. Cook and stir over medium heat until jelly is melted. Remove from heat.

To Prepare Vegetables: In a small covered saucepan cook onions in a small amount of boiling water for 3 minutes. Add squash; cook for 1 minute more. Drain.

To Prepare Meat: Trim fat from steak. Cut steak into 1-inch cubes. On eight 6- to 8-inch metal skewers, alternately thread onions, squash, steak, tomatillos, and red or green sweet pepper.

To Cook by Direct Grill Method: Place kabobs on the grill rack of an uncovered grill. Grill directly over medium coals for 12 to 14 minutes for medium doneness (160°), turning once and brushing occasionally with glaze the last 5 minutes of grilling.

To Serve: If desired, serve kabobs with hot polenta and any remaining glaze. Makes 4 servings.

Nutrition Facts per serving: 444 cal., 11 g total fat (4 g sat. fat), 76 mg chol., 71 mg sodium, 61 g carbo., 27 g pro.

chili-rubbed steaks

Down in the Rio Grande Valley they called it comino and put it on everything. No question—cumin in the rub makes these steaks great.

2   12-ounce beef rib eye steaks, cut 1 inch thick

1   tablespoon chili powder

1   tablespoon olive oil

1¹/₂ teaspoons dried oregano, crushed

¹/₂ teaspoon salt

¹/₂ teaspoon ground cumin

To Prepare Meat: Trim fat from steaks. Place steaks in a single layer in a shallow dish. For rub, in a small bowl combine the chili powder, oil, oregano, salt, and cumin. Spoon mixture over steaks; rub in with your fingers. Cover and marinate in the refrigerator for 1 to 2 hours.

To Cook by Direct Grill Method: Grill steaks on the rack of an uncovered grill directly over medium coals 12 to 15 minutes for medium doneness (160°), turning once halfway through grilling.

To Serve: Cut steaks into serving-size pieces. Makes 4 servings.

Nutrition Facts per serving: 323 cal., 16 g total fat (5 g sat. fat), 92 mg chol., 376 mg sodium, 1 g carbo., 42 g pro.

grilled basil burgers

Basil, garlic, and Parmesan cheese add an unexpected zing to these lunch or dinnertime burgers.

1 beaten egg

²/₃ cup chopped onion

¹/₂ cup grated Parmesan cheese

¹/₄ cup snipped fresh basil or
     1 tablespoon dried basil, crushed

¹/₄ cup catsup

2 cloves garlic, minced

¹/₄ teaspoon salt

¹/₄ teaspoon black pepper

1 pound lean ground beef

1 pound ground raw turkey

8 hamburger buns

8 tomato slices

To Prepare Meat Mixture: In a medium mixing bowl combine egg, onion, Parmesan cheese, basil, catsup, garlic, salt, and pepper. Add ground beef and turkey and mix well. Shape mixture into approximately eight ¾-inch-thick patties.

To Cook by Indirect Grill Method: In a covered grill arrange preheated coals around drip pan. Test for medium heat above the pan. Place meat on the grill over the drip pan. Cover and grill for 20 to 24 minutes or until done (160°), turning once halfway through grilling time.

To Cook by Direct Grill Method: Grill meat on the grill rack of an uncovered grill directly over medium coals for 14 to 18 minutes or until done (160°), turning once halfway through grilling time.

To Serve: Split buns and toast on the grill. Serve patties in buns with tomato slices. Makes 8 servings.

Nutrition Facts per serving: 333 cal., 14 g total fat (5 g sat. fat), 88 mg chol., 570 mg sodium, 25 g carbo., 25 g pro.

tips from the kitchen

toasting buns, rolls, and bread A little extra touch, like toasting the bun or bread of a sandwich, makes an already great sandwich even better. Take advantage of your hot grill and leave your kitchen cool by toasting the buns on the grill. To grill, place bun or roll halves or bread split side down on a grill rack directly over the coals. Grill about one minute or until lightly toasted.

five-spice burgers

Teriyaki sauce and five-spice powder lend the very American burger an Oriental flair.

1   beaten egg

¹/₄   cup fine dry bread crumbs

¹/₄   cup finely shredded carrot

1   tablespoon milk

1   clove garlic, minced

¹/₂   teaspoon five-spice powder

¹/₈   teaspoon salt

1   pound lean ground beef

¹/₄   cup teriyaki sauce

4   hamburger buns

4   large spinach leaves

To Prepare Meat Mixture: In a medium mixing bowl combine egg, bread crumbs, carrot, milk, garlic, five-spice powder, and salt. Add ground beef and mix well. Shape mixture into four ¾-inch-thick patties.

To Marinate: Place patties in a shallow baking dish. Pour teriyaki sauce over patties. Cover and refrigerate for 1 to 2 hours, turning once. Remove patties from baking dish and pat dry with paper towels; discard marinade.

To Cook by Indirect Grill Method: In a covered grill arrange preheated coals around a drip pan. Test for medium heat above the pan. Place meat on the grill rack over the drip pan. Cover and grill for 20 to 24 minutes or until done (160°), turning once halfway through grilling time.

To Cook by Direct Grill Method: Grill meat on an uncovered grill directly over medium coals for 14 to 18 minutes or until done (160°), turning once halfway through grilling time.

To Serve: Split the buns and toast on the grill. Serve patties in buns with spinach. Makes 4 servings.

Nutrition Facts per serving: 348 cal., 14 g total fat (5 g sat. fat), 125 mg chol., 571 mg sodium, 26 g carbo., 27 g pro.

double-beef burgers

Hidden within these burgers are all the makings of a Reuben sandwich—corned beef, cabbage, and rye bread. If desired, top with slices of Swiss cheese just before taking off the grill.

1   beaten egg

1   2¹/₂-ounce package very thinly sliced fully cooked corned beef, chopped

¹/₃ cup finely chopped cabbage

¹/₄ cup soft rye bread crumbs (about ¹/₂ slice)

¹/₂ teaspoon caraway seed

¹/₄ teaspoon salt

1   pound lean ground beef

8   slices rye bread

3   tablespoons horseradish mustard

4   small kale, cabbage, or lettuce leaves

To Prepare Meat Mixture: In a medium mixing bowl combine egg, corned beef, cabbage, bread crumbs, caraway seed, and salt. Add ground beef and mix well. Shape mixture into four ¾-inch-thick patties.

To Cook by Indirect Grill Method: In a covered grill arrange preheated coals around a drip pan. Test for medium heat above the pan. Place meat on the grill rack over the drip pan. Cover and grill for 20 to 24 minutes or until done (160°), turning once halfway through grilling time.

To Cook by Direct Grill Method: Grill meat on the grill rack of an uncovered grill directly over medium coals for 14 to 18 minutes or until done (160°), turning once halfway through grilling time.

To Serve: Toast the bread slices on the grill. Spread toasted bread slices with horseradish mustard. Serve patties on bread slice; top each burger with a kale leaf and second bread slice. Makes 4 servings.

Nutrition Facts per serving: 376 cal., 16 g total fat (5 g sat. fat), 135 mg chol., 883 mg sodium, 29 g carbo., 31 g pro.

spanish meat loaves

Serve these diminutive, green-olive-stuffed loaves with Barcelona-style Spanish rice or thinly sliced potatoes and onions cooked in a foil pack alongside them on the grill.

1 slightly beaten egg

3/4 cup quick-cooking rolled oats

1/2 cup pimiento-stuffed green olives, sliced

1/4 cup snipped fresh parsley

1/4 cup tomato paste

1/4 teaspoon black pepper

1 pound lean ground beef

1/4 cup jalapeño pepper jelly or apple jelly, melted

1 medium tomato, chopped

1/3 cup chunky salsa

1/4 cup chopped, seeded cucumber

2 tablespoons sliced pimiento-stuffed green olives (optional)

To Prepare Meat: In a medium bowl combine the egg, rolled oats, the ½ cup olives, the parsley, tomato paste, and pepper. Add ground beef; mix well. Shape into four 4×2½×1-inch meat loaves.

To Cook by Direct Grill Method: Place meat loaves on the grill rack of an uncovered grill. Grill directly over medium coals for 16 to 18 minutes or until internal temperature reaches 160°, turning once. Brush with melted jelly; grill for 2 minutes more.

For Relish: In a small bowl combine the tomato, salsa, cucumber, and, if desired, the 2 tablespoons olives.

To Serve: Serve the meat loaves with relish. Makes 4 servings.

Nutrition Facts per serving: 362 cal., 16 g total fat (5 g sat. fat), 125 mg chol., 479 mg sodium, 31 g carbo., 26 g pro.

marinated blade steaks

The savory marinade and sauce also taste great on beef flank steak.

1   4-ounce can chopped green chile peppers (undrained)

$^1/_3$ cup red wine vinegar

$^1/_4$ cup olive oil or cooking oil

1   tablespoon hot-style mustard

2   teaspoons dried Italian seasoning, crushed

2   cloves garlic, minced

4   pork shoulder blade steaks, cut $^1/_2$ inch thick (2 to $2^1/_2$ pounds total)

$^1/_2$ cup tomato sauce

1   tablespoon honey

For Marinade: In a small mixing bowl combine green chile peppers, red wine vinegar, olive oil or cooking oil, mustard, Italian seasoning, and garlic.

To Prepare Meat: Trim fat from meat. Place steaks in a plastic bag set into a shallow dish. Pour marinade over steaks in bag. Seal bag and turn steaks to coat well. Marinate in the refrigerator for 6 to 24 hours, turning bag occasionally. Remove steaks from bag, reserving $^1/_4$ cup of the marinade.

For Sauce: In a small saucepan combine tomato sauce, honey, and $^1/_4$ cup reserved marinade. Bring to boiling; boil at least 1 minute. Remove from heat; set aside.

To Cook by Indirect Grill Method: In a covered grill arrange preheated coals around a drip pan. Test for medium-high heat above the pan. Place steaks on the grill rack over the drip pan. Cover and grill for 24 to 28 minutes or until pork is tender and juices run clear, brushing occasionally with sauce halfway through the grilling time. Pass remaining sauce with the meat. Makes 4 servings.

Nutrition Facts per serving: 544 cal., 38 g total fat (10 g sat. fat), 154 mg chol., 489 mg sodium, 10 g carbo., 41 g pro.

peanut-sauced ribs

Peanut butter, apple juice concentrate, teriyaki sauce, and curry powder are the secrets to the spicy, Indian-inspired brushing sauce.

3 tablespoons hot water

¹/₃ cup peanut butter

¹/₂ of a 6-ounce can (¹/₃ cup) apple juice concentrate, thawed

3 tablespoons cooking oil

2 tablespoons teriyaki sauce

1 tablespoon curry powder

2 cloves garlic, minced

Several dashes bottled hot pepper sauce

4 pounds pork loin back ribs or meaty spareribs

For Sauce: In a small mixing bowl gradually stir hot water into peanut butter. (The mixture will stiffen at first.) Stir in apple juice concentrate, cooking oil, teriyaki sauce, curry powder, garlic, and hot pepper sauce until mixture is smooth. Set sauce aside.

To Prepare Meat: Cut the ribs into serving-size pieces.

To Cook by Indirect Grill Method: In a covered grill arrange preheated coals around a drip pan. Test for medium heat above the pan. Place ribs on the grill rack over the drip pan. Cover and grill for 1¼ to 1½ hours or until ribs are tender and juices run clear, brushing occasionally with sauce the last 10 minutes of grilling. Pass any remaining sauce. Makes 6 servings.

Nutrition Facts per serving: *647 cal., 50 g total fat (16 g sat. fat), 143 mg chol., 413 mg sodium, 11 g carbo., 38 g pro.*

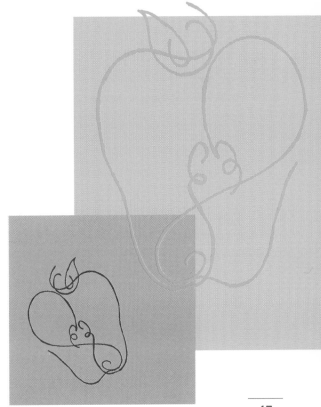

spiced-and-smoked ribs

Hickory chips add depth and flavor to these succulent pork ribs.

4 cups hickory chips

4 pounds meaty pork spareribs or pork loin back ribs

1 tablespoon brown sugar

1 teaspoon five-spice powder

$1/2$ teaspoon paprika

$1/4$ teaspoon salt

$1/4$ teaspoon celery seed

$1/4$ teaspoon black pepper

$1/2$ cup catsup

2 tablespoons light molasses

1 tablespoon lemon juice

1 tablespoon soy sauce

Several dashes bottled hot pepper sauce

To Prepare Wood Chips: At least 1 hour before grilling, soak wood chips in enough water to cover. Drain chips before using.

To Precook Ribs: Cut ribs into serving-size pieces. Place ribs in a Dutch oven. Add enough water to cover ribs.

Bring to boiling; reduce heat. Cover and simmer for 30 minutes. Drain ribs; cool ribs slightly.

For Seasoning Rub: In a small mixing bowl combine brown sugar, five-spice powder, paprika, salt, celery seed, and pepper. When ribs are cool enough to handle, rub seasoning mixture over ribs.

For Glaze: In a small mixing bowl combine catsup, molasses, lemon juice, soy sauce, and hot pepper sauce. Set aside.

To Cook by Indirect Grill Method: In a covered grill arrange preheated coals around a drip pan. Test for medium heat above the pan. Sprinkle the drained wood chips onto the preheated coals. Place precooked ribs on the grill rack over the drip pan. Cover and grill for 45 to 50 minutes or until ribs are tender and juices run clear, brushing occasionally with the glaze the last 15 minutes of grilling. Makes 6 servings.

Nutrition Facts per serving: 520 cal., 36 g total fat (14 g sat. fat), 143 mg chol., 610 mg sodium, 13 g carbo., 35 g pro.

thai-coconut ribs

These grilled ribs marinate in a spicy and gingery coconut-milk sauce that will send your taste buds to Thailand.

1 cup coconut milk

3 tablespoons brown sugar

3 tablespoons soy sauce

1 tablespoon grated fresh ginger

1 teaspoon finely shredded lime peel

1 tablespoon lime juice

4 cloves garlic, minced

1 teaspoon crushed red pepper

4 pounds pork loin back ribs

For Marinade: In a small bowl combine coconut milk, brown sugar, soy sauce, ginger, lime peel, lime juice, garlic, and red pepper. Set aside.

To Prepare Meat: Trim fat from ribs. Cut ribs into 6 serving-size pieces. Place ribs in a plastic bag set in a shallow bowl. Pour marinade over ribs in bag. Seal bag and turn ribs to coat well. Marinate in the refrigerator for 8 to 24 hours, turning bag occasionally. Drain ribs, reserving marinade.

To Cook by Indirect Grill Method: In a covered grill arrange preheated coals around a drip pan. Test for medium heat above the pan. Place ribs, bone side down, on grill rack over drip pan. Cover and grill for 1¼ to 1½ hours or until ribs are tender and juices run clear, brushing frequently with marinade the first hour of grilling. Discard remaining marinade. Makes 6 servings.

Nutrition Facts per serving: 431 cal., 32 g total fat (16 g sat. fat), 99 mg chol., 607 mg sodium, 9 g carbo., 25 g pro.

oriental pork chops

Super easy and simply sensational. Marinate the chops one night, and grill them the next.

$^1/_3$ cup soy sauce

$^1/_4$ cup cooking oil

1   tablespoon finely shredded orange peel

$^1/_4$ cup orange juice

$^1/_4$ cup finely chopped green sweet pepper

1   tablespoon brown sugar

2   teaspoons ground ginger

1   teaspoon ground turmeric

4   pork loin or rib chops, cut $1^1/_4$ inches thick (about $2^1/_4$ pounds total)

4   cups hickory wood chips or mesquite wood chips (optional)

For Marinade: In a small mixing bowl combine soy sauce, cooking oil, orange peel, orange juice, green sweet pepper, brown sugar, ginger, and turmeric.

To Prepare Meat: Trim fat from meat. Place pork chops in a plastic bag set into a deep bowl. Pour marinade over chops in bag. Seal bag and turn chops to coat well. Marinate in the refrigerator for 6 to 24 hours, turning bag occasionally. Remove chops from bag, reserving marinade. Chill marinade while grilling meat.

tips from the kitchen

smoke 'em Tossing wood chips on your grill gives foods a wood-smoked aroma and flavor. Generally, wood chips need to be soaked for about an hour in enough water to cover them. Afterward, drain the wood chips well and toss onto hot coals. Good choices for wood chips include mesquite, alder, hickory, oak, and sweetish fruitwoods such as apple, cherry, and peach.

To Prepare Wood Chips: If using, at least 1 hour before grilling, soak wood chips in enough water to cover. Drain the chips before using.

To Cook by Indirect Grill Method: In a covered grill arrange preheated coals around a drip pan. Test for medium heat above the pan. If using, sprinkle 1 cup of the drained wood chips onto the preheated coals. Place pork chops on the grill rack over the drip pan. Cover and grill for 35 to 50 minutes or until juices run clear (160°), turning once and brushing with reserved marinade after 25 minutes. Discard remaining marinade. Add additional drained wood chips, if using, as necessary. Makes 4 servings.

Nutrition Facts per serving: 466 cal., 30 g total fat (8 g sat. fat), 116 mg chol., 1448 mg sodium, 9 g carbo., 38 g pro.

cajun-style pork chops

Three kinds of ground pepper add a cajun-style kick to these pork chops.

1 teaspoon onion powder

¹/₄ to **¹/₂** teaspoon ground white pepper

¹/₄ to **¹/₂** teaspoon ground red pepper

¹/₄ to **¹/₂** teaspoon black pepper

¹/₄ teaspoon salt

4 pork loin or rib chops, cut 1¹/₄ inches thick (about 2¹/₄ pounds total)

For Seasoning Rub: In a small mixing bowl combine onion powder, white pepper, red pepper, black pepper, and salt.

To Prepare Meat: Trim fat from meat. Rub both sides of each pork chop with the seasoning rub.

To Cook by Indirect Grill Method: In a covered grill arrange preheated coals around a drip pan. Test for medium heat above the pan. Place the pork chops on the grill rack over the drip pan. Cover and grill for 35 to 45 minutes or until the juices run clear (160°), turning once.

To Cook by Direct Grill Method: Grill pork chops on the grill rack of an uncovered grill directly over medium coals for 25 to 35 minutes or until juices run clear (160°), turning once. Makes 4 servings.

Nutrition Facts per serving: *207 cal., 11 g total fat (4 g sat. fat), 77 mg chol., 192 mg sodium, 1 g carbo., 24 g pro.*

sesame pork ribs

Ginger and sesame—two terrific tastes make for one great rib recipe.

¹/₄ cup water

¹/₄ cup soy sauce

¹/₄ cup dry sherry

2 to 2¹/₂ pounds pork country-style ribs

¹/₄ cup soy sauce

¹/₄ cup dry sherry

1 tablespoon sugar

1 tablespoon lemon juice

2 teaspoons sesame seed, toasted and crushed

1 teaspoon grated fresh ginger or ¹/₄ teaspoon ground ginger

1 teaspoon toasted sesame oil

For Marinade: In a small mixing bowl combine water, ¼ cup soy sauce, and ¼ cup sherry.

To Prepare Ribs: Place ribs in a plastic bag set into a deep bowl. Pour marinade over ribs in bag. Seal bag and turn ribs to coat well. Marinate in the refrigerator for 6 to 24 hours, turning bag occasionally. Remove ribs from bag; discard marinade.

For Sauce: In a small mixing bowl combine ¼ cup soy sauce, ¼ cup sherry, the sugar, lemon juice, sesame seed, ginger, and sesame oil. Set aside.

To Cook by Indirect Grill Method: In a covered grill arrange preheated coals around a drip pan. Test for medium heat above the pan. Place ribs on the grill rack over the drip pan. Cover and grill for 1½ to 2 hours or until ribs are tender and juices run clear, brushing occasionally with the sauce. Makes 4 servings.

Nutrition Facts per serving: 463 cal., 28 g total fat (9 g sat. fat), 145 mg chol., 1,159 mg sodium, 7 g carbo., 39 g pro.

curried mustard pork chops

Serve these curry-and-mustard-flavored chops with lots of steamed rice.

¹/₂ cup spicy brown mustard

¹/₄ cup dry white wine

1 tablespoon curry powder

1 tablespoon olive oil

1 green onion, sliced

1 clove garlic, minced

¹/₄ to ¹/₂ teaspoon crushed red pepper

4 boneless pork loin chops, cut 1 inch thick

For Marinade: In a small bowl stir together brown mustard, wine, curry powder, oil, green onion, garlic, and red pepper.

To Prepare Meat: Trim fat from chops. Place chops in a plastic bag set in a shallow bowl. Pour marinade over chops. Seal bag and turn chops to coat well. Marinate in the refrigerator for 6 to 24 hours, turning bag occasionally. Drain chops, reserving marinade.

To Cook by Indirect Grill Method: In a covered grill arrange preheated coals around a drip pan. Test for medium heat above the pan. Place chops on grill rack over the drip pan. Cover and grill for 30 to 35 minutes or until juices run clear, turning and brushing with marinade halfway through grilling. Makes 4 servings.

Nutrition Facts per serving: 225 cal., 13 g total fat (4 g sat. fat), 64 mg chol., 353 mg sodium, 2 g carbo., 22 g pro.

lamb chops with rosemary

Make any occasion special with a dinner of lamb chops delicately seasoned with rosemary.

¹/₃ cup dry white wine

¹/₃ cup lemon juice

¹/₄ cup finely chopped onion

3 tablespoons olive oil or cooking oil

1 tablespoon snipped fresh rosemary or
    1 teaspoon dried rosemary, crushed

¹/₂ teaspoon salt

¹/₄ teaspoon black pepper

8 lamb loin chops, cut 1 inch thick
    (about 2¹/₂ pounds total)

Fresh rosemary sprigs (optional)

For Marinade: In a small mixing bowl combine wine, lemon juice, onion, olive oil, snipped or dried rosemary, salt, and pepper.

To Prepare Meat: Trim fat from meat. Place lamb chops in a plastic bag set into a deep bowl. Pour marinade over chops in bag. Seal bag and turn chops to coat well. Marinate in the refrigerator for 6 to 24 hours, turning bag occasionally. Remove chops from bag, reserving the marinade.

To Cook by Indirect Grill Method: In a covered grill arrange preheated coals around a drip pan. Test for medium heat above the pan. Place lamb chops on the grill rack over the drip pan. Cover and grill for 18 to 20 minutes for medium doneness (160°), brushing with reserved marinade halfway through grilling time.

To Cook by Direct Grill Method: Grill lamb chops on the grill rack of an uncovered grill directly over medium coals for 14 to 16 minutes for medium doneness (160°), turning chops once and brushing with reserved marinade halfway through grilling time.

To Serve: If desired, garnish with fresh rosemary. Makes 4 servings.

Nutrition Facts per serving: 455 cal., 27 g total fat (8 g sat. fat), 148 mg chol., 380 mg sodium, 3 g carbo., 45 g pro.

marinated leg of lamb

$^1/_2$ cup cooking oil

$^1/_3$ cup lemon juice

$^1/_4$ cup finely chopped onion

  2 tablespoons snipped fresh parsley

  1 teaspoon salt

$^1/_2$ teaspoon dried thyme, crushed

$^1/_2$ teaspoon dried basil, crushed

$^1/_4$ teaspoon dried tarragon, crushed

  1 4-pound boneless leg of lamb, rolled and tied

For Marinade: In a small mixing bowl combine cooking oil, lemon juice, onion, parsley, salt, thyme, basil, and tarragon.

To Prepare Meat: Trim fat from meat. Place meat in a plastic bag set into a shallow dish. Pour marinade over meat in bag. Seal bag and turn meat to coat well. Marinate in the refrigerator for 6 to 24 hours, turning bag occasionally. Remove meat from bag, reserving marinade. Chill marinade while grilling meat. Insert meat thermometer near the center of roast.

To Cook by Indirect Grill Method: In a covered grill arrange preheated coals around a drip pan. Test for medium heat above the pan. Place meat on a rack in a roasting pan on the grill rack. Cover and grill for 1¾ to 2¼ hours for medium-rare (145°) or 2 to 2½ hours for medium (160°), brushing occasionally with reserved marinade during the first 1½ hours. Remove strings and slice meat to serve. Makes 16 servings.

Nutrition Facts per serving: 214 cal., 15 g total fat (5 g sat. fat), 66 mg chol., 114 mg sodium, 0 g carbo., 18 g pro.

fish & seafood

**Caramelized Salmon
with Citrus Salsa**
(recipe, page 58)

tuna steaks with hot chile pepper sauce

Prefer a hotter sauce to eat with the fish? Then be sure to include the jalapeño pepper seeds when finely chopping the pepper.

1/3 cup mayonnaise or salad dressing

1 jalapeño pepper, finely chopped*

1 tablespoon Dijon-style mustard

1 teaspoon lemon juice

Dash ground red pepper

1 tablespoon olive oil or cooking oil

4 6-ounce fresh or frozen tuna or halibut steaks, cut 1 inch thick (thawed, if frozen)

For Sauce: In a small mixing bowl combine mayonnaise or salad dressing, jalapeño pepper, Dijon-style mustard, and lemon juice. Cover and chill in the refrigerator until serving time.

To Prepare Fish: Stir ground red pepper into oil. Rinse fish; pat dry with paper towels. Brush both sides of tuna or halibut steaks with olive oil or cooking oil mixture.

To Cook by Indirect Grill Method: In a covered grill arrange preheated coals around a drip pan. Test for medium heat above the pan. Place fish on the greased grill rack over the drip pan. Cover and grill for 8 to 12 minutes or just until fish begins to flake easily, turning once and brushing with olive oil or cooking oil mixture halfway through grilling time.

To Cook by Direct Grill Method: Grill fish on the greased rack of an uncovered grill directly over medium coals for 8 to 12 minutes or until fish begins to flake easily, turning once and brushing with olive oil or cooking oil mixture halfway through grilling time.

To Serve: Serve grilled fish with sauce. Makes 4 servings.

Nutrition Facts per serving: 462 cal., 31 g total fat (5 g sat. fat), 81 mg chol., 333 mg sodium, 1 g carbo., 44 g pro.

*Note: When seeding and chopping a fresh chile pepper, protect your hands with plastic gloves. The oils in the pepper can irritate your skin. Also, avoid direct contact with your eyes. When finished with the chile pepper, wash your hands thoroughly.

swordfish à la thyme

A crisp lettuce salad and buttered French bread wrapped in foil and grilled alongside the fish would complement this thyme-enhanced dish.

1/4   cup olive oil or cooking oil

1/4   cup white wine vinegar

2   green onions, thinly sliced (1/4 cup)

1   teaspoon dried thyme, crushed

4   6-ounce fresh or frozen swordfish or halibut steaks, cut 1 inch thick (thawed, if frozen)

   Lemon wedges

For Marinade: In a small mixing bowl combine olive oil or cooking oil, white wine vinegar, green onions, and thyme.

To Prepare Fish: Rinse fish; pat dry with paper towels. Place fish in a plastic bag set into a deep bowl. Pour marinade over fish in bag. Seal bag and turn fish to coat well. Marinate in the refrigerator for 1 hour, turning bag occasionally. Remove fish from bag, reserving marinade.

To Cook by Indirect Grill Method: In a covered grill arrange preheated coals around a drip pan. Test for medium heat above the pan. Place fish on the greased grill rack over the drip pan. Cover and grill for 8 to 12 minutes or just until fish begins to flake easily, turning once and brushing with reserved marinade halfway through grilling time.

To Cook by Direct Grill Method: Grill fish on the greased rack of an uncovered grill directly over medium coals for 8 to 12 minutes or just until fish begins to flake easily, turning once and brushing with reserved marinade halfway through grilling time.

To Serve: Garnish with lemon wedges. Makes 4 servings.

Nutrition Facts per serving: 329 cal., 20 g total fat (4 g sat. fat), 67 mg chol., 153 mg sodium, 2 g carbo., 34 g pro.

tips from the kitchen

is it done yet? *Testing fish for doneness can be a tricky job even for expert grillers. A few tips will help: If grilling fish with the skin on, let the skin brown and begin to pull away from the grill before trying to turn the fish. Grill fish until it is opaque through the thickest part. Don't cook until it is dry or it will turn tough. The best test of all is to take a quick peek at the thickest part of the fish with a fork. When done, the fish will flake easily.*

caramelized salmon with citrus salsa

Because jalapeños vary in their level of heat, you might want to taste the salsa before adding all of the jalapeño. (Recipe pictured on pages 54-55.)

2	tablespoons sugar
1¹/₂	teaspoons finely shredded orange peel
1	teaspoon salt
¹/₄	teaspoon ground black pepper
1	1¹/₂-pound fresh or frozen salmon fillet (with skin), 1 inch thick (thawed, if frozen)
1	teaspoon finely shredded orange peel
2	oranges, peeled, sectioned, and coarsely chopped
1	cup chopped fresh pineapple or canned crushed pineapple, drained
2	tablespoons snipped fresh cilantro
1	tablespoon finely chopped shallot
1	jalapeño pepper, seeded and finely chopped

For Rub: In a small bowl stir together sugar, the 1½ teaspoons orange peel, the salt, and pepper. Set aside.

To Prepare Fish: Rinse fish; pat dry with paper towels. Place fish, skin side down, in a shallow dish. Sprinkle rub evenly over fish (not on skin side); rub in with your fingers. Cover and marinate in the refrigerator for 8 to 24 hours. Drain fish, discarding liquid.

For Salsa: In a small bowl stir together the 1 teaspoon orange peel, the oranges, pineapple, cilantro, shallot, and jalapeño pepper. Cover and chill in the refrigerator until ready to serve or up to 24 hours.

To Cook by Indirect Grill Method: In a covered grill arrange preheated coals around a drip pan. Test for medium heat above the pan. Place fish, skin side down, on greased grill rack over drip pan. Cover and grill about 12 minutes or until fish flakes easily.

To Serve: Cut fish into 4 serving-size pieces, cutting to but not through the skin. Carefully slip a metal spatula between fish and skin, lifting fish up and away from skin. Serve fish with salsa. Makes 4 servings.

Nutrition Facts per serving: 145 cal., 4 g total fat (1 g sat. fat), 20 mg chol., 424 mg sodium, 10 g carbo., 17 g pro.

garden-stuffed fish steaks

These swordfish steaks, an elegant entrée for guests, are stuffed with vegetables, bread crumbs, and cheese, then grilled to perfection.

$1/2$ cup coarsely shredded carrot

$1/4$ cup sliced green onions

1 clove garlic, minced

2 tablespoons margarine or butter

1 small tomato, seeded and chopped

2 tablespoons fine dry seasoned bread crumbs

2 tablespoons grated Parmesan cheese

4 5- to 6-ounce fresh or frozen swordfish or tuna steaks, cut 1 inch thick (thawed, if frozen)

For Stuffing: In a small saucepan cook carrot, green onions, and garlic in hot margarine or butter until vegetables are tender. Remove from heat. Add tomato, bread crumbs, and cheese; toss lightly to mix.

To Prepare Fish: Rinse fish; pat dry with paper towels. If necessary, remove bones and skin. Make a pocket in each steak by cutting horizontally from one side almost through to the other side. Spoon about ¼ cup stuffing into each pocket. Secure the openings with toothpicks.

To Cook by Direct Grill Method: Place fish on the greased grill rack of an uncovered grill. Grill directly over medium-hot coals for 14 to 18 minutes or until fish flakes easily, gently turning once halfway through grilling. Makes 4 servings.

Nutrition Facts per serving: *293 cal., 16 g total fat (4 g sat. fat), 58 mg chol., 352 mg sodium, 5 g carbo., 30 g pro.*

red snapper with herb-pecan crust

Thanks to its nutty crust, this grilled fish stays juicy. For a lovely combination, serve this with grilled summer squash brushed with lemon butter and a simple toss of steamed rice.

4　5- or 6-ounce fresh or frozen red snapper or salmon fillets (with skin) $^1/_2$ to $^3/_4$ inch thick

$^1/_3$　cup finely chopped pecans

2　tablespoons fine dry bread crumbs

2　tablespoons margarine or butter, softened

1　tablespoon snipped fresh Italian flat-leaf parsley

1　finely shredded lemon peel

2　cloves garlic, minced

1　teaspoon sugar

$^1/_4$　teaspoon salt

$^1/_8$　teaspoon black pepper

Dash ground red pepper

Lemon wedges (optional)

To Prepare Fish: Thaw fish, if frozen. Rinse fish; pat dry with paper towels. In a small bowl combine pecans, bread crumbs, margarine or butter, parsley, lemon peel, garlic, salt, black pepper, and red pepper.

To Cook by Direct Grill Method: Place fish, skin sides down, on the greased rack of an uncovered grill directly over medium coals. Spoon the pecan mixture over the fish; spread slightly. Grill until fish flakes easily when tested with a fork. Allow 4 to 6 minutes per $^1/_2$-inch thickness of the fish.

To Serve: Transfer to a serving platter. If desired, serve with lemon wedges. Makes 4 servings.

Nutrition Facts per serving: 268 cal., 14 g total fat (2 g sat. fat), 52 mg chol., 287 mg sodium, 7 g carbo., 30 g pro.

tips from the kitchen

handle with care
Fish is a great candidate for the grill, if you're willing to take a little extra care to keep it from falling apart. It helps to place fish on a double layer of heavy-duty foil and to use a wide spatula if you must turn it, or to place it in a grill basket. Also, cut slits in the foil before placing fish on foil. This will allow the juices to drain so the fish doesn't poach in them. Be sure to lightly grease or brush the foil or grill basket with cooking oil or lightly coat it with nonstick cooking spray before adding the fish. Firmer-textured fish steaks can be grilled directly on top of a greased grill rack.

halibut steaks with green onion sauce

Chervil lends its sweet licoricelike flavor to the savory green onion sauce.

6 green onions, sliced ($3/4$ cup)

1 clove garlic, minced

2 tablespoons margarine or butter

2 teaspoons all-purpose flour

$1/2$ teaspoon dried chervil, crushed

$1/2$ teaspoon instant chicken bouillon granules

$1/8$ teaspoon salt

$3/4$ cup milk

4 6-ounce fresh or frozen halibut or tuna steaks, cut 1 inch thick (thawed, if frozen)

2 tablespoons olive oil or cooking oil

For Sauce: In a small saucepan cook green onions and garlic in margarine or butter until onion is tender but not brown. Stir in flour, chervil, chicken bouillon granules, and salt. Add milk all at once. Cook and stir over medium heat until thickened and bubbly. Cook and stir for 1 minute more. Keep sauce warm while grilling fish.

To Prepare Fish: Rinse fish; pat dry with paper towels. Brush both sides of halibut or tuna steaks with olive oil or cooking oil.

To Cook by Indirect Grill Method: In a covered grill arrange preheated coals around a drip pan. Test for medium heat above the pan. Place fish on the greased grill rack over the drip pan. Cover and grill for 8 to 12 minutes or until fish begins to flake easily, turning once and brushing with olive oil or cooking oil halfway through grilling time.

To Cook by Direct Grill Method: Grill fish on the greased rack of an uncovered grill directly over medium coals for 8 to 12 minutes or until fish begins to flake easily, turning once and brushing with olive oil or cooking oil halfway through grilling time.

To Serve: Serve sauce over grilled fish steaks. Makes 4 servings.

Nutrition Facts per serving: 327 cal., 17 g total fat (3 g sat. fat), 58 mg chol., 357 mg sodium, 4 g carbo., 37 g pro.

tropical halibut steaks

A sprinkling of toasted coconut accents the subtle curry and fruit flavors of the marinade and sauce. Sea bass or snapper could substitute for the halibut.

$^1/_3$ cup pineapple-orange juice

$^1/_3$ cup soy sauce

$^1/_4$ teaspoon curry powder

  4   6-ounce fresh or frozen halibut steaks, cut 1 inch thick (thawed, if frozen)

  1   8-ounce can pineapple chunks

$^1/_4$ of a medium cantaloupe or $^1/_2$ of a papaya (1 cup)

     Dash curry powder

  2   teaspoons cornstarch

  2   tablespoons toasted coconut

For Marinade: In a small mixing bowl combine pineapple-orange juice, soy sauce, and curry powder.

To Prepare Fish: Rinse fish; pat dry with paper towels. Place fish in a plastic bag set into a deep bowl. Pour marinade over fish in bag. Seal bag and turn fish to coat well. Marinate in the refrigerator for 1 hour, turning bag occasionally. Remove fish from bag, reserving marinade.

To Prepare Fruit Sauce: Drain pineapple chunks, reserving juice. Peel and seed cantaloupe or papaya. Finely chop fruit. In a small saucepan combine chopped pineapple, cantaloupe or papaya, and the curry powder.

Add enough water to reserved pineapple juice to make $^1/_2$ cup liquid. Stir in cornstarch. Add pineapple juice mixture to fruit mixture in saucepan. Cook and stir over medium heat until thickened and bubbly. Cook and stir for 2 minutes more. Keep warm.

To Cook by Indirect Grill Method: In a covered grill arrange preheated coals around a drip pan. Test for medium heat above the pan. Place fish on the greased grill rack over the drip pan. Cover and grill for 8 to 12 minutes or until fish begins to flake easily, turning once and brushing with reserved marinade halfway through grilling time.

To Cook by Direct Grill Method: Grill fish on the greased rack of an uncovered grill directly over medium coals for 8 to 12 minutes or until fish begins to flake easily, turning once and brushing with reserved marinade halfway through grilling time.

To Serve: Spoon fruit sauce over grilled halibut. To garnish, sprinkle with toasted coconut. Makes 4 servings.

Nutrition Facts per serving: 256 cal., 5 g total fat (1 g sat. fat), 55 mg chol., 351 mg sodium, 15 g carbo., 36 g pro.

mahi mahi with vegetable slaw

Fresh cilantro makes all the difference in this flavorful fish dish.

- **1** teaspoon finely shredded lime peel (set aside)
- **1/4** cup lime juice
- **1/4** cup snipped fresh cilantro
- **3** tablespoons olive oil
- **1** tablespoon honey
- **1** jalapeño pepper, seeded and finely chopped
- **3** cloves garlic, minced
- **1/8** teaspoon salt
- **4** 5- to 6-ounce fresh or frozen mahi mahi or pike fillets, 1/2 to 3/4 inch thick (thawed, if frozen)
- **1 1/2** cups packaged shredded cabbage with carrot (coleslaw mix)
- **1** cup shredded jicama

For Dressing: In a small bowl combine lime juice, cilantro, oil, honey, jalapeño pepper, garlic, and salt; divide in half. Stir lime peel into one portion of dressing. Set both halves aside.

To Prepare Fish: Rinse fish; pat dry with paper towels. Place fish in a shallow dish. Pour dressing with lime peel over fish; turn fish to coat. Cover; marinate at room temperature for 30 minutes. Drain fish, discarding marinade. Place fish in a greased grill basket, tucking under any thin edges.

For Slaw: In a medium bowl combine cabbage mixture and jicama. Pour remaining dressing over slaw; toss to coat. Cover and chill until ready to serve.

To Cook by Direct Grill Method: Place fish in a greased grill basket, tucking under any thin edges. Grill on uncovered grill directly over medium coals until fish flakes easily (allow 4 to 6 minutes per 1/2-inch thickness of fish), turning basket once halfway through grilling.

To Serve: Serve fish with slaw. Makes 4 servings.

Nutrition Facts per serving: 276 cal., 10 g total fat (1 g sat. fat), 67 mg chol., 130 mg sodium, 12 g carbo., 34 g pro.

63

grilled trout with fennel stuffing

Feel free to substitute pike, cod, or another favorite mild-flavored fish.

2 heads fennel

1 clove garlic, minced

1/4 teaspoon salt

1/8 teaspoon black pepper

2 tablespoons margarine or butter

1 tablespoon fresh snipped parsley

3 tablespoons margarine or butter

1 tablespoon lemon juice

1/2 teaspoon dried rosemary, crushed

Dash black pepper

4 8- to 10-ounce fresh or frozen dressed trout or other fish (thawed, if frozen)

Lemon wedges (optional)

Fresh parsley sprigs (optional)

For Stuffing: Discard top and outer pieces of fennel. Chop fennel heads. (Should have about 2½ cups.) In a medium saucepan cook and stir fennel, garlic, salt, and the ⅛ teaspoon pepper in the 2 tablespoons margarine or butter for 10 minutes or until fennel is tender but not brown. Stir in parsley. Set aside.

For Sauce: In a small saucepan combine the 3 tablespoons margarine or butter, lemon juice, rosemary, and the dash pepper. Heat through.

To Prepare Fish: Rinse fish; pat dry with paper towels. Spoon one-fourth of the stuffing into each fish cavity. Skewer the cavity closed with wooden toothpicks. Brush fish with sauce. Cut several slits in a piece of heavy foil large enough to hold fish. Grease foil and place fish on it.

To Cook by Indirect Grill Method: In a covered grill arrange preheated coals around a drip pan. Test for medium heat above the pan. Place foil with fish on the grill rack over the drip pan. Cover and grill for 15 to 20 minutes or until fish begins to flake easily, brushing frequently with sauce.

To Serve: Remove toothpicks. If desired, garnish with lemon and parsley sprigs. Makes 4 servings.

Nutrition Facts per serving: 409 cal., 22 g total fat (4 g sat. fat), 130 mg chol., 376 mg sodium, 3 g carbo., 47 g pro.

apple-stuffed trout

If all the stuffing doesn't fit into the fish cavities, place any extra stuffing in a foil pouch. Heat on the grill the last few minutes of cooking.

1/4 cup dried apple

1 1/2 cups corn bread stuffing mix

2 tablespoons chopped hazelnuts (filberts) or pecans, toasted

1 tablespoon thinly sliced green onion

1 tablespoon margarine or butter, melted

1/4 cup water

1/4 teaspoon instant chicken bouillon granules

4 8- to 10-ounce fresh or frozen dressed trout or other fish (thawed, if frozen)

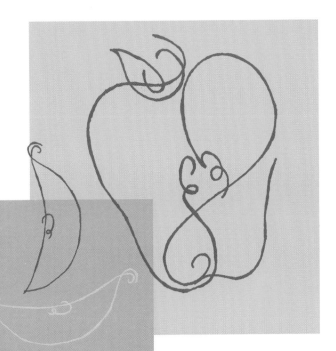

For Stuffing: In a small mixing bowl combine snipped dried apple and enough boiling water to cover. Let stand 5 minutes. Drain. In a medium mixing bowl stir together the drained apple, stuffing mix, hazelnuts or pecans, green onion, and margarine or butter. In another small bowl stir together the ¼ cup water and the bouillon granules. Toss stuffing mixture with the water-bouillon mixture. Add an additional 1 tablespoon water if mixture is too dry.

To Prepare Fish: Rinse fish; pat dry with paper towels. Spoon one-fourth of the stuffing into each fish cavity. Skewer the cavity closed with wooden toothpicks. Cut several slits in a piece of heavy foil large enough to hold fish. Grease foil and place fish on it.

To Cook by Indirect Grill Method: In a covered grill arrange preheated coals around a drip pan. Test for medium heat above the pan. Place foil with fish on the grill rack over the drip pan. Cover and grill for 20 to 25 minutes or just until fish begins to flake easily. Remove toothpicks before serving. Makes 4 servings.

Nutrition Facts per serving: 456 cal., 14 g total fat (2 g sat. fat), 130 mg chol., 514 mg sodium, 29 g carbo., 51 g pro.

scallops and sweet peppers

Use the larger sea scallops instead of the smaller bay or calico scallops when preparing this recipe. For a pretty presentation, use a combination of red and yellow sweet peppers.

2 tablespoons lemon juice

2 tablespoons finely chopped shallot (about 1 shallot)

1 tablespoon olive oil or cooking oil

1 tablespoon water

1/8 teaspoon salt

Dash black pepper

1 pound fresh or frozen sea scallops (thawed, if frozen)

1 medium red and/or yellow sweet pepper

1 cup fresh pea pods

For Marinade: In a small mixing bowl combine the lemon juice, shallot, olive oil or cooking oil, water, salt, and the pepper.

To Prepare Seafood: Rinse scallops; pat dry with paper towels. Cut any large scallops in half. Place scallops in a plastic bag set into a deep bowl. Pour marinade over scallops in bag. Seal bag and turn scallops to coat well. Marinate in the refrigerator for 1 to 2 hours, turning bag occasionally.

To Prepare Vegetables: Cut red sweet pepper into 1-inch pieces. Remove tips and strings from pea pods. Cut pea pods in half crosswise. Add pepper pieces and pea pods to marinated scallops; toss to mix.

To Prepare Mixture: Tear off a 36×18-inch piece of heavy foil. Fold in half to make a double thickness of foil that measures 18×18 inches. Place scallop and vegetable mixture with marinade in the center of the foil. Bring up two opposite edges of foil and seal with a double fold. Then fold remaining ends to completely enclose the scallops and vegetables, leaving space for steam to build.

To Cook by Indirect Grill Method: In a covered grill arrange preheated coals around a drip pan. Test for medium heat above the pan. Place the foil packet on the grill rack not over the coals. Cover and grill about 25 minutes or until scallops turn opaque, turning once.

To Cook by Direct Grill Method: Grill foil packet on the grill rack of an uncovered grill directly over medium coals about 25 minutes or until scallops turn opaque, turning once.

To Serve: Serve scallops and vegetables with a slotted spoon. Makes 4 servings.

Nutrition Facts per serving: *123 cal., 4 g total fat (0 g sat. fat), 34 mg chol., 238 mg sodium, 6 g carbo., 16 g pro.*

garlic and shrimp pasta toss

As any Italian cook knows, garlic, butter, shrimp, and pasta were made for each other. But using roasted garlic can make the best even better.

1 pound fresh or frozen large shrimp in shells (thawed, if frozen)

1 large garlic bulb

1 tablespoon olive oil

2 tablespoons lemon juice

1 red or yellow sweet pepper, quartered lengthwise

1 onion, cut into ¹/₂-inch slices

3 cups packaged dried cavatelli (curled shells) or bow tie pasta (farfalle) (about 8 ounces)

2 tablespoons butter, softened

¹/₂ teaspoon salt

¹/₂ teaspoon black pepper

¹/₃ cup shredded Asiago or Parmesan cheese

To Prepare Shrimp: Peel and devein shrimp, leaving tails intact. Rinse shrimp; pat dry with paper towels. Cover and refrigerate until ready to grill.

For Garlic: With a sharp knife, cut off the top ¹/₂ inch from garlic bulb to expose the ends of the individual cloves. Leaving garlic bulb whole, remove any loose, papery outer layers. Fold an 18×9-inch piece of heavy foil in half to make a 9-inch square. Place garlic bulb, cut side up, in center of foil. Drizzle bulb with 1¹/₂ teaspoons of the oil. Bring up opposite edges of foil and seal with a double fold. Fold remaining edges together to enclose garlic, leaving room for steam to build.

To Cook By Indirect Grill Method: In a covered grill arrange preheated coals around a drip pan. Test for medium heat above the pan. Place garlic on greased grill rack over drip pan. Cover and grill for 30 minutes. Thread shrimp onto long metal skewers, leaving a ¹/₄-inch space between pieces. In a small bowl combine the remaining oil and 1 tablespoon of the lemon juice; brush over shrimp and vegetables. Add skewers to grill over drip pan; add vegetables to grill directly over coals. Cover and grill for 8 to 10 minutes more or until garlic is soft, shrimp are opaque, and vegetables are tender, turning shrimp and vegetables once halfway through grilling. Remove from grill. Cool garlic and vegetables slightly. Coarsely chop vegetables.

While shrimp and vegetables are grilling, cook pasta according to package directions; drain. Return pasta to hot pan.

To Serve: Squeeze garlic pulp into a small bowl. Thoroughly mash garlic pulp. Add butter, salt, and pepper; mix well. In a large bowl combine pasta and garlic mixture; toss to coat. Add shrimp, vegetables, remaining lemon juice, and cheese; toss gently to mix. Serve immediately. Makes 4 servings.

Nutrition Facts per serving: 404 cal., 16 g total fat (7 g sat. fat), 174 mg chol., 567 mg sodium, 44 g carbo., 21 g pro.

raspberry shrimp salad

When the temperature soars, plan a luncheon or supper around this refreshing salad. Round out the meal with warm rolls or crusty French bread slices and a luscious chocolate dessert.

2 cups fresh raspberries

1/4 cup olive oil or salad oil

1/4 cup white wine vinegar or white vinegar

1 teaspoon sugar

1/2 teaspoon finely shredded orange peel

1/4 teaspoon dry mustard

1 cup fresh pea pods

1 pound fresh or frozen jumbo shrimp in shells (16 per pound) (thawed, if frozen)

6 cups torn red-tip leaf lettuce

For Vinaigrette: In a blender container or food processor bowl combine 1 cup of the raspberries, olive oil or salad oil, white wine vinegar or white vinegar, sugar, orange peel, and dry mustard. Cover and blend or process until smooth. Set aside.

To Prepare Vegetable: Remove tips and strings from pea pods. In a small saucepan cook pea pods, covered, in a small amount of boiling water for 2 to 4 minutes or until crisp-tender. Drain. Set aside.

To Prepare Seafood: Peel and devein shrimp. To butterfly shrimp, make a deeper slit along its back; do not cut all the way through the shellfish. Lay the shrimp on a flat surface so that the sides open to resemble a butterfly. On 4 long metal skewers, loosely thread shrimp, leaving about 1/4-inch between pieces.

To Cook by Indirect Grill Method: In a covered grill arrange preheated coals around a drip pan. Test for medium heat above the pan. Place skewers on the grill rack over the drip pan. Cover and grill for 8 to 10 minutes or until shrimp turn opaque.

To Cook by Direct Grill Method: Grill skewers on the grill rack of an uncovered grill directly over medium coals for 6 to 8 minutes or until shrimp turn opaque, turning once.

To Serve: Arrange torn lettuce and the pea pods on 4 dinner plates. Divide grilled shrimp among the plates. Top each plate with 1/4 cup of the remaining raspberries. Serve with vinaigrette. Makes 4 servings.

Nutrition Facts per serving: 246 cal., 15 g total fat (2 g sat. fat), 131 mg chol., 158 mg sodium, 14 g carbo., 17 g pro.

grilled crab legs with dipping sauce

The king crab legs called for in this recipe come precooked and only need to be heated on the grill before serving.

12 fresh or frozen cooked crab legs (thawed, if frozen) (about 3 pounds)

2 tablespoons margarine or butter

1 green onion, sliced (2 tablespoons)

1 teaspoon dried dillweed

1 tablespoon margarine or butter

1/2 cup dairy sour cream

1/4 cup mayonnaise or salad dressing

1/8 teaspoon ground red pepper

To Prepare Seafood: Split whole crab legs in half lengthwise. To split them, use kitchen shears to cut shell along top and bottom, then cut the meat in between. In a small saucepan melt the 2 tablespoons margarine or butter.

For Sauce: In a small saucepan cook green onion and dillweed in the 1 tablespoon margarine or butter until onion is just tender. Stir in sour cream, mayonnaise or salad dressing, and red pepper. Heat mixture through. Do not boil.

To Cook by Indirect Grill Method: In a covered grill arrange preheated coals around a drip pan. Test for medium heat above the pan. Place split crab legs, shell side down, on the grill rack over the drip pan. Cover and grill for 10 to 12 minutes or until heated through, brushing with the melted margarine or butter halfway through grilling time.

To Cook by Direct Grill Method: Place split crab legs, shell side down, on the grill rack of an uncovered grill directly over medium coals. Grill for 8 minutes or until heated through, brushing with the melted margarine or butter halfway through grilling time.

To Serve: Serve crab legs with sauce. Makes 4 servings.

Nutrition Facts per serving: 375 cal., 28 g total fat (7 g sat. fat), 96 mg chol., 1,715 mg sodium, 2 g carbo., 29 g pro.

appetizers, sides, & desserts

Three-Way Chicken Wings
(recipe, page 72)

three-way chicken wings

Brush the chicken pieces with one of these three sauces the last 5 minutes of grilling so that the sauce doesn't burn. (Recipe pictured on pages 70-71.)

1 cup chili sauce

$^1/_2$ cup currant jelly, melted

2 tablespoons snipped fresh chives

2 teaspoons prepared mustard

$1^1/_3$ cups chicken broth

$^1/_2$ cup hot-style mustard

4 teaspoons cornstarch

2 teaspoons soy sauce

$^2/_3$ cup packed brown sugar

$^2/_3$ cup unsweetened pineapple juice

$^2/_3$ cup red wine vinegar

2 tablespoons cornstarch

2 tablespoons soy sauce

$^1/_4$ teaspoon ground ginger

24 chicken wings (about $4^1/_2$ pounds), wing tips tucked under

For Easy Barbecue Sauce: In a small mixing bowl stir together chili sauce, currant jelly, chives, and mustard.

For Spicy Mustard Sauce: In a small saucepan stir together chicken broth, mustard, cornstarch, and the 2 teaspoons soy sauce. Cook and stir until thickened and bubbly. Cook and stir for 2 minutes more.

For Sweet-and-Sour Sauce: In a small saucepan stir together brown sugar, pineapple juice, red wine vinegar, cornstarch, the 2 tablespoons soy sauce, and ginger. Cook and stir until thickened and bubbly. Cook and stir for 2 minutes more.

To Cook by Indirect Grill Method: In a covered grill arrange preheated coals around a drip pan. Test for medium heat above the pan. Place chicken wings on the grill rack over the drip pan. Cover and grill for 25 to 30 minutes or until chicken is tender and no longer pink, brushing wings with the 3 sauces (8 wings per sauce) the last 5 minutes of cooking.

To Cook by Direct Grill Method: Grill chicken wings on the grill rack of an uncovered grill directly over medium coals about 20 minutes or until chicken is tender and no longer pink, turning occasionally and brushing wings with the 3 sauces (8 wings per sauce) the last 5 minutes of cooking.

To Serve: Transfer remaining sauces to separate serving bowls and use for dipping sauces. Makes 24 wings.

Nutrition Facts per serving: 482 cal., 19 g total fat (5 g sat. fat), 82 mg chol., 1,174 mg sodium, 46 g carbo., 28 g pro.

grilled quesadillas

The pepper cheese makes these appetizer-size servings plenty hot. For a milder flavor, use the plain Monterey Jack cheese in the filling. Sour cream and/or guacamole and salsa add extra flavor.

6   7-inch flour tortillas

2   tablespoons cooking oil

¹/₂   cup salsa

1¹/₂   cups shredded Monterey Jack cheese with jalapeño peppers or shredded Monterey Jack cheese (6 ounces)

Dairy sour cream, guacamole, and/or salsa

Fresh cilantro sprigs (optional)

For Quesadillas: Brush one side of 3 of the tortillas with some of the cooking oil. Place tortillas, oil side down, on a large baking sheet. Spread salsa over each tortilla on baking sheet. Sprinkle each with cheese. Top with remaining tortillas. Brush top tortillas with remaining oil.

To Cook by Indirect Grill Method: In a covered grill arrange preheated coals around a drip pan. Test for medium heat above the pan. Place quesadillas on the grill rack not over coals. Cover and grill 4 to 5 minutes or until cheese begins to melt and tortillas start to brown, turning once.

To Cook by Direct Grill Method: Grill quesadillas on the grill rack of an uncovered grill directly over medium coals for 3 to 4 minutes or until cheese begins to melt and tortillas start to brown, turning once.

To Serve: Cut quesadillas into wedges. Top each with a dab of sour cream, guacamole, and/or salsa, and, if desired, cilantro. Makes 6 servings.

Nutrition Facts per serving: 289 cal., 19 g total fat (9 g sat. fat), 34 mg chol., 236 mg sodium, 20 g carbo., 10 g pro.

caramelized onion and cheese bites

This accompaniment can be prepared up to an hour in advance and only takes a few minutes to cook alongside your meat on the grill.

1 large onion, halved and thinly sliced

1 tablespoon olive oil or cooking oil

1/3 cup coarsely chopped walnuts

1 teaspoon sugar

1 tablespoon herb mustard or Dijon-style mustard

16 1/4-inch-thick slices baguette French bread or other long, thin firm bread

1/2 cup freshly grated Parmesan or Romano cheese

For Onion: In a large skillet cook the sliced onion in hot oil about 3 minutes or just until tender. Add the walnuts and the sugar. Continue to cook and stir about 5 minutes more or until the onion is slightly caramelized and walnuts are lightly toasted. Stir in the mustard.

For Bread: Spoon some of the onion mixture on each of the bread slices. Sprinkle with the cheese. If desired, cover bread slices and let stand at room temperature up to 1 hour.

To Cook by Direct Grill Method: Place bread slices, onion side up, on the grill rack of an uncovered grill. Grill directly over medium-high coals about 2 minutes or just until bottoms are toasted and slices are heated through. Watch bread slices carefully the last 30 seconds to avoid overbrowning. Makes 8 servings.

Nutrition Facts per serving: 205 cal., 8 g total fat (1 g sat. fat), 5 mg chol., 360 mg sodium, 25 g carbo., 8 g pro.

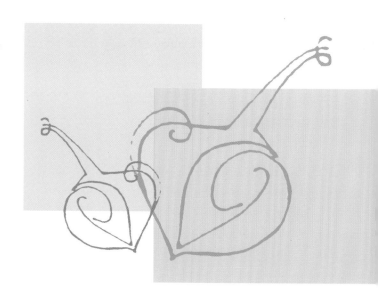

piquant broccoli and olives

You probably don't think of broccoli when you consider vegetables for the grill. But grilling gives it a great smoky flavor worth trying.

¹/₂ of a 2-ounce can anchovy fillets, drained and finely chopped (optional)

2 tablespoons snipped fresh oregano or Italian flat parsley

2 tablespoons red wine vinegar

2 tablespoons olive oil

5 cloves garlic, minced

¹/₂ teaspoon crushed red pepper

Dash salt

3¹/₂ cups broccoli flowerets

¹/₂ cup pitted ripe olives

For Marinade: In a small bowl whisk together anchovies (if using), oregano, red wine vinegar, olive oil, garlic, red pepper, and salt. Set aside.

To Prepare Broccoli: In a large saucepan bring a small amount of water to boiling; add broccoli flowerets. Simmer, covered, for 2 minutes. Drain well. In a medium bowl combine broccoli and olives. Pour the marinade over the broccoli and olives. Marinate at room temperature for 10 minutes, stirring occasionally. Drain broccoli and olives; discard marinade. On long metal skewers alternately thread broccoli flowerets and olives.

To Cook by Direct Grill Method: Place kabobs on the grill rack of an uncovered grill. Grill directly over medium coals for 6 to 8 minutes or until broccoli is lightly browned and tender, turning occasionally. Makes 4 servings.

Nutrition Facts per serving: 91 cal., 8 g total fat (1 g sat. fat), 0 mg chol., 125 mg sodium, 6 g carbo., 3 g pro.

grilled german potato salad

Heat this salad favorite alongside meat or poultry as it cooks. It goes great with sausages, chops, steaks, burgers, or chicken.

3   medium potatoes (about 1 pound), cut into ³/₄-inch cubes

4   slices bacon

1   medium onion, chopped (¹/₂ cup)

¹/₂ cup finely chopped celery

1   tablespoon all-purpose flour

1   tablespoon sugar

¹/₂ teaspoon salt

¹/₂ teaspoon celery seed

¹/₄ teaspoon dry mustard

¹/₈ teaspoon black pepper

¹/₃ cup water

¹/₄ cup cider vinegar

To Prepare Vegetable: In a large covered saucepan cook the potatoes in a small amount of boiling lightly salted water for 10 minutes. Drain potatoes well; cool slightly. Set aside.

For Dressing: In a large skillet cook bacon until crisp. Drain the bacon, reserving 2 tablespoons of the drippings. Crumble bacon; set aside. Cook onion and celery in the reserved drippings until tender. Stir in flour, sugar, salt, celery seed, mustard, and pepper. Add water and cider vinegar all at once. Cook and stir until thickened and bubbly. Remove from heat. Stir in crumbled bacon.

To Prepare Packet: Tear off a 36×18-inch piece of heavy foil. Fold in half to make a double thickness of foil that measures 18×18 inches. Place potatoes in the center of the foil. Pour dressing over potatoes. Bring up two opposite edges of foil and seal with a double fold. Then fold remaining ends to completely enclose the potato mixture, leaving space for steam to build.

To Cook by Direct Grill Method: Place foil packet on the grill rack of an uncovered grill. Grill directly over medium to medium-high coals for 15 to 20 minutes or until heated through. Makes 4 servings.

Nutrition Facts per serving: 243 cal., 10 g total fat (4 g sat. fat), 11 mg chol., 391 mg sodium, 35 g carbo., 5 g pro.

summer squash casserole

This colorful dish teams wonderfully with Savory Grilled Turkey (see recipe, page 27) or any grilled poultry dish.

2 pounds yellow summer squash and/or zucchini

1/4 cup chopped onion

1 10³/₄-ounce can condensed cream of chicken soup

1 8-ounce carton dairy sour cream

2 medium carrots, shredded (about 1 cup)

1/2 of an 8-ounce package (2 cups) herb-seasoned stuffing mix

1/4 cup margarine or butter, melted

To Prepare Vegetables: Slice yellow squash and/or zucchini in half lengthwise. Then cut halves into ½-inch-thick slices (about 7 cups). Cook the yellow squash and/or zucchini and onion, covered, in a small amount of boiling water about 3 minutes or until crisp-tender. Drain well. In an extra-large mixing bowl stir together soup, sour cream, and carrots. Stir in squash and onion. Set aside.

To Prepare Bread Mixture: In a medium mixing bowl toss the stuffing mix with the melted margarine or butter.

To Prepare Packet: Tear off two 24×18-inch pieces of heavy foil. Make a double thickness of foil that measures 24×18 inches. Arrange half of the bread mixture on the foil in a 12×7-inch rectangle. Spoon vegetable mixture over bread mixture on foil. Top with remaining bread mixture. Bring up two opposite edges of foil and seal with a double fold. Then fold remaining ends to completely enclose the mixture, leaving space for steam to build.

To Cook by Direct Grill Method: Place foil packet on the grill rack of an uncovered grill. Grill directly over medium to medium-high coals about 20 minutes or until heated through. Makes 8 servings.

Nutrition Facts per serving: 233 cal., 15 g total fat (6 g sat. fat), 16 mg chol., 694 mg sodium, 21 g carbo., 5 g pro.

tips from the kitchen

wrap it up Preparing side dishes in foil packets is a slick trick that helps you make the best use of your grill. Place the packet alongside the meat as it cooks. If the meat takes longer to cook than the packet, keep the prepared packet in the refrigerator until it's time to add it to the grill. You may need to add a few extra minutes of grilling time to make sure the chilled side dish is heated. Be sure to open the packets carefully as the steam that builds in the sealed packet is very hot.

cheese and peas potatoes

This hearty, family-style side dish is an easy, cheesy, vegetable mixture for four.

1   4-ounce container cheese spread with mild Mexican flavor ($^1/_2$ cup)

$^1/_2$ of a 16-ounce package (2 cups) loose-pack frozen hash brown potatoes with onion and peppers

$^3/_4$ cup loose-pack frozen peas

$^1/_4$ cup chopped salami

To Prepare Vegetables: Spoon cheese spread into a medium saucepan; cook and stir over low heat until melted. Stir potatoes, peas, and salami into cheese.

To Prepare Packet: Tear off two 22×18-inch pieces of heavy foil. Make a double thickness of foil that measures 22×18. Place the potato mixture in center of the foil. Bring up two opposite edges of foil and seal with a double fold. Then fold remaining ends to completely enclose the potato mixture, leaving space for steam to build.

To Cook by Direct Grill Method: Place foil packet on the grill rack of an uncovered grill. Grill directly over medium to medium-high coals for 17 to 25 minutes or until heated through, turning frequently. Makes 4 servings.

Nutrition Facts per serving: 201 cal., 10 g total fat (5 g sat. fat), 23 mg chol., 617 mg sodium, 20 g carbo., 9 g pro.

southwestern grilled corn

Remember to turn the foil-wrapped ears as they grill to get corn that's evenly cooked. For those who like more seasoning, sprinkle corn with additional salt and red pepper to taste.

¹/₃ cup margarine or butter

2 tablespoons snipped fresh cilantro or parsley

¹/₄ teaspoon salt

¹/₄ teaspoon ground red pepper

6 fresh ears of corn

For Seasoning: In a small saucepan melt margarine or butter. Stir in cilantro or parsley, salt, and ground red pepper.

To Prepare Vegetable: Remove the husks from fresh ears of corn. Scrub ears with a stiff brush to remove silks. Rinse ears; pat dry with paper towels. Place each ear of corn on a piece of heavy foil. Brush ears with seasoning mixture. Wrap corn securely in foil.

To Grill by Direct Grill Method: Place corn on the grill rack of an uncovered grill. Grill directly over medium to medium-high coals about 20 minutes or until kernels are tender, turning frequently. Makes 6 servings.

Nutrition Facts per serving: 173 cal., 11 g total fat (2 g sat. fat), 0 mg chol., 220 mg sodium, 19 g carbo., 3 g pro.

herbed sourdough bread

For make-ahead convenience, assemble, wrap, and refrigerate this bread ahead of time. About 15 minutes before serving, add the foil-wrapped package to the grill and heat through.

1/2 cup margarine or butter, softened

2 tablespoons snipped chives or finely chopped green onion

2 tablespoons snipped fresh parsley

4 teaspoons snipped fresh tarragon or **3/4** teaspoon dried tarragon, crushed

1 16-ounce loaf unsliced sourdough bread

For Spread: In a small mixing bowl stir together margarine or butter, chives, parsley, and tarragon.

For Bread: Cut bread crosswise into 1-inch-thick slices, cutting to but not through bottom crust. Spread cut surfaces with spread. Tear off a 48×18-inch piece of heavy foil. Fold in half to make a double thickness of foil that measures 24×18 inches. Place bread in the center of the foil. Bring up two opposite edges of foil and seal with a double fold. Then fold remaining ends to completely enclose the bread, leaving space for steam to build.

To Cook by Direct Grill Method: Place bread on the grill rack of an uncovered grill. Grill directly over medium to medium-high coals about 15 minutes or until heated through. Makes 12 servings.

Nutrition Facts per serving: 174 cal., 9 g total fat (2 g sat. fat), 0 mg chol., 298 mg sodium, 19 g carbo., 4 g pro.

nectarine sundaes

A nectarine transforms into the most amazing delicacy when grilled and brushed with honey. Choose nectarines that are fully ripe, but still firm.

2 medium nectarines, halved lengthwise and pitted

1 tablespoon margarine or butter, melted

2 tablespoons honey or flavored honey

1/8 teaspoon ground nutmeg

1/2 pint (1 cup) vanilla ice cream

1 cup blueberries

1 cup sliced strawberries

1/4 cup crushed amaretti cookies, crushed gingersnaps, or granola

To Prepare Nectarines: Brush cut sides of nectarines with margarine or butter.

To Cook by Direct Grill Method: Place nectarines on the grill rack of an uncovered grill. Grill directly over medium coals for 10 to 12 minutes or until nectarines are tender, turning and brushing once with honey halfway through grilling.

To Serve: Sprinkle cut sides of nectarines with nutmeg. Place in dessert dishes, cut sides up. Top each nectarine half with some of the ice cream, blueberries, and strawberries. Sprinkle with crushed cookies or granola. Makes 4 servings.

Nutrition Facts per serving: 212 cal., 7 g total fat (3 g sat. fat), 15 mg chol., 93 mg sodium, 36 g carbo., 2 g pro.

caramel apple slices

If you prefer, serve these luscious apples with slices of pound cake or sugar cookies in place of the ice cream.

- **1/3** cup packed brown sugar
- **2** tablespoons margarine or butter, softened
- **2** tablespoons light corn syrup
- **1** teaspoon ground cinnamon
- **3** cups sliced, peeled cooking apples (3 medium)
- **1** pint vanilla ice cream

For Topping: In a small mixing bowl stir together brown sugar, margarine or butter, corn syrup, and cinnamon. Set aside.

To Prepare Packet: Tear off a 36×18-inch piece of heavy foil. Fold in half to make a double thickness of foil that measures 18×18 inches. Place apples in the center of the foil. Drizzle with topping. Bring up two opposite edges of foil and seal with a double fold. Then fold remaining ends to completely enclose the apples, leaving space for steam to build.

To Cook by Indirect Grill Method: In a covered grill arrange preheated coals around a drip pan. Test for medium heat above the pan. Place foil packet on grill rack not over coals. Cover and grill for 30 to 35 minutes or until apples are tender.

To Cook by Direct Grill Method: Place foil packet on the grill rack of an uncovered grill. Grill directly over medium coals for 15 to 20 minutes or until apples are tender.

To Serve: Serve apple mixture warm with ice cream. Makes 4 to 6 servings.

Nutrition Facts per serving: *353 cal., 13 g total fat (6 g sat. fat), 30 mg chol., 139 mg sodium, 59 g carbo., 3 g pro.*

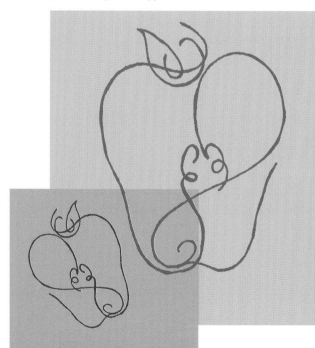

chocolate-sauced dessert kabobs

Leftover chocolate sauce makes a tasty topping for ice cream.

- ³/₄ cup semisweet chocolate pieces
- ¹/₄ cup margarine or butter
- ²/₃ cup sugar
- 1 5-ounce can (²/₃ cup) evaporated milk
- 2 medium ripe nectarines or peaches
- 2 ripe bananas
- ¹/₂ of a 10³/₄-ounce frozen loaf pound cake
- 6 whole strawberries

For Sauce: In a heavy small saucepan melt chocolate pieces and margarine or butter over low heat. Add the sugar. Gradually stir in milk. Bring to boiling; reduce heat. Boil gently over low heat for 8 minutes, stirring frequently. Remove from heat. Set aside.

To Prepare Kabobs: Peel peaches, if using. Remove pits from nectarines or peaches; cut fruit into wedges. Cut the bananas into 1-inch pieces. Cut the cake into 1-inch cubes. Remove stems from strawberries. On 6 long skewers, alternately thread peaches or nectarines, bananas, and cake cubes. Add one strawberry to each skewer.

To Cook by Direct Grill Method: Place kabobs on the grill rack of an uncovered grill. Grill directly over medium coals about 5 minutes or until cake is toasted, turning once.

To Serve: For each serving, push fruit and cake from skewer onto a dessert plate. Drizzle with chocolate sauce. (Store any remaining sauce tightly covered in the refrigerator for another use.) Makes 6 servings.

Nutrition Facts per serving: 455 cal., 23 g total fat (7 g sat. fat), 59 mg chol., 162 mg sodium, 63 g carbo., 5 g pro.

Honey-Peach Sauce and
Mango and Pepper Barbecue Sauce
(recipes, pages 90 and 91)

lemon-rosemary marinade

Use this marinade for about 1¹/₂ pounds of fish, such as salmon, halibut, shark, swordfish, or tuna steaks.

1 teaspoon finely shredded lemon peel

¹/₃ cup lemon juice

¹/₄ cup olive oil or cooking oil

¹/₄ cup white wine Worcestershire sauce

1 tablespoon sugar

1 tablespoon snipped fresh rosemary, basil, or thyme or 1 teaspoon dried rosemary, basil, or thyme, crushed

¹/₄ teaspoon salt

¹/₈ teaspoon black pepper

For Marinade: In a small mixing bowl combine all ingredients. Place 1 to 1½ pounds fish in a plastic bag set into a shallow bowl. Pour marinade over fish in bag.

Seal bag and turn fish to coat well. Marinate in the refrigerator for 1 to 2 hours, turning bag occasionally. Remove fish from bag, reserving marinade if desired.

To Cook: Grill fish over medium coals until fish flakes easily. (Timings will vary depending on the type of fish.) If desired, brush with marinade halfway through grilling. (Discard remaining marinade.) Makes about ¾ cup (about 12 tablespoons).

Nutrition Facts per serving: 49 cal., 5 g total fat (1 g sat. fat), 0 mg chol., 87 mg sodium, 3 g carbo., 0 g pro.

red wine and peppercorn marinade

A great marinade for 1 to 2 pounds of meat, such as beef sirloin steak or beef cubes for kabobs. Be sure to begin marinating the meat ahead of time to enhance the flavor.

²/₃ cup dry red wine

¹/₂ cup cooking oil

2 tablespoons cracked whole black pepper

2 tablespoons snipped fresh thyme or 1 teaspoon dried thyme, crushed

2 bay leaves

¹/₄ teaspoon salt

For Marinade: In a small mixing bowl combine all ingredients. Place 1 to 2 pounds beef steaks or beef cubes in a plastic bag set into a deep bowl. Pour marinade over meat in bag. Seal bag and turn meat to coat well. Marinate in the refrigerator for 6 to 24 hours, turning bag occasionally. Remove meat from bag, reserving marinade if desired.

To Cook: Grill meat over medium coals until medium doneness (160°). (Timings will vary depending on the cut of beef.) If desired, brush with marinade halfway through grilling. (Discard remaining marinade.) Makes about 1¼ cups (about 20 tablespoons).

Nutrition Facts per serving: 55 cal., 5 g total fat (1 g sat. fat), 0 mg chol., 27 mg sodium, 0 g carbo., 0 g pro.

tips from the **kitchen**

marinating tips When brushing on marinade used for meat, poultry, or fish, be sure to brush on only during the early stages of cooking. The marinade has raw meat juices in it that need to be thoroughly cooked. Marinate foods in the refrigerator; don't let them stand at room temperature. Marinades are not reusable. Discard any leftover marinade not to be boiled and served with the meat.

garlic and basil marinade

Try this flavorful marinade with about 2 pounds of meaty chicken pieces, such as breasts, thighs, and drumsticks.

²/₃ cup dry white wine or white wine vinegar

¹/₃ cup olive oil or cooking oil

1 green onion, sliced (2 tablespoons)

2 tablespoons snipped fresh basil, oregano, or rosemary, or 1¹/₂ teaspoons dried basil, oregano, or rosemary, crushed

1 teaspoon sugar

2 cloves garlic, minced

For Marinade: In a small mixing bowl combine all ingredients. Place 2 to 2½ pounds meaty chicken pieces in a plastic bag set into a deep bowl or shallow dish.

Pour marinade over chicken in bag. Seal bag and turn chicken to coat well. Marinate in the refrigerator for 6 to 24 hours, turning bag occasionally. Remove chicken from bag, reserving marinade if desired.

To Cook: Grill chicken over medium coals for 35 to 45 minutes or until chicken is tender and no longer pink. If desired, brush with marinade halfway through grilling. (Discard remaining marinade.) Makes about 1 cup. (about 16 tablespoons).

Nutrition Facts per serving: 48 cal., 5 g total fat (1 g sat. fat), 0 mg chol., 1 mg sodium, 0 g carbo., 0 g pro.

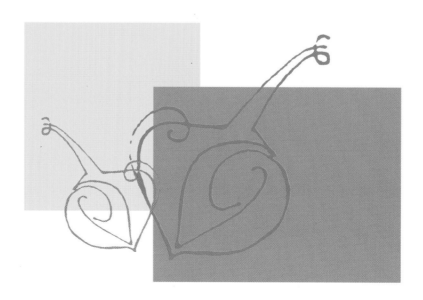

plum-good barbecue sauce

Just like the name says—this sauce is based on a can of purple plums. It's a good choice to use on your favorite pieces of poultry.

1 medium onion, chopped (¹/₂ cup)

1 tablespoon margarine or butter

1 17-ounce can whole, unpitted purple plums

1 6-ounce can frozen lemonade concentrate, thawed

¹/₄ cup catsup

2 tablespoons soy sauce

2 teaspoons prepared mustard

1 teaspoon ground ginger

1 teaspoon Worcestershire sauce

For Sauce: In a medium saucepan cook onion in margarine or butter until tender. Drain plums, reserving syrup. Remove pits from plums; discard pits. In a blender container or food processor bowl combine plums and reserved syrup. Cover and blend or process until smooth. Stir plum puree, lemonade concentrate, catsup, soy sauce, mustard, ginger, and Worcestershire sauce into the onion mixture. Bring to boiling; reduce heat. Simmer, uncovered, for 10 to 15 minutes or until desired consistency, stirring occasionally.

To Cook: Grill chicken over medium coals for 35 to 45 minutes or until chicken is tender and no longer pink. If desired, brush with sauce halfway through grilling. (Discard remaining marinade.) Makes about 3 cups. (about 48 tablespoons).

Nutrition Facts per serving: 21 cal., 0 g total fat (0 g sat. fat), 0 mg chol., 66 mg sodium, 5 g carbo., 0 g pro.

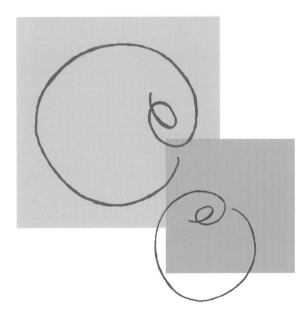

honey-peach sauce

Nothing says summer like a perfect peach. Here's a sauce to highlight the season's bounty. Plus, this sauce pairs well with pork, beef, or chicken. (Recipe pictured on pages 84-85.)

4 medium peaches

2 tablespoons lemon juice

2 tablespoons honey

$^1/_2$ teaspoon cracked pepper

1 to 2 teaspoons snipped fresh thyme

For Sauce: Peel and cut up 3 of the peaches. Place in a blender container. Add lemon juice, honey, and pepper. Cover and blend until smooth. Transfer to a medium saucepan. Bring to boiling; reduce heat. Simmer, uncovered, about 15 minutes or until slightly thickened, stirring occasionally. Remove from heat. Peel and finely chop the remaining peach; stir into the sauce. Stir in thyme. Brush over pork, beef, or poultry the last 15 minutes of grilling. Pass any remaining sauce. Makes about 1¾ cups (about 28 tablespoons).

Nutrition Facts per serving: 15 cal., 0 g total fat (0 g sat. fat), 0 mg chol., 0 mg sodium, 4 g carbo., 0 g pro.

mango and pepper barbecue sauce

What starts out as a chunky salsa you could serve alongside your grilled food winds up being pureed into a terrific barbecue sauce for the top of it. (Recipe pictured on pages 84-85.)

- **2** cups chopped sweet red pepper
- **1/2** cup chopped onion
- **2** tablespoons cooking oil
- **2** medium mangoes, seeded, peeled, and chopped (2 cups)
- **1/4** cup packed brown sugar
- **2** tablespoons rice vinegar
- **1/2** teaspoon crushed red pepper
- **1/4** teaspoon salt
- **2** tablespoons finely chopped green onion

tips from the kitchen

mango seeds
Removing the large seed of a mango takes a little cutting expertise, but don't be intimidated. It's best to place the fruit on its blossom end and align a sharp knife slightly off-center on the stem end of the fruit. Slice down through the peel and flesh, next to the pit. Repeat on the other side of the seed. Cut off remaining flesh around the seed. Remove the peel and cut the mango into pieces as directed in your recipe.

For Sauce: In a large skillet cook the chopped sweet red pepper and onion in hot oil just until tender. Stir in the mangoes, brown sugar, vinegar, crushed red pepper, and salt. Bring to boiling; reduce heat. Simmer, uncovered, about 10 minutes or until mangoes are tender. Cool mixture slightly. Transfer mixture to a blender container or food processor bowl. Cover and blend or process until nearly smooth. Stir in the green onion. Brush over chicken, shrimp, fish, or pork the last 10 minutes of grilling. Pass any remaining sauce. Makes about 2½ cups (about 40 tablespoons).

Nutrition Facts per serving: 19 cal., 1 g total fat (0 g sat. fat), 0 mg chol., 14 mg sodium, 3 g carbo., 0 g pro.

green tangy avocado salsa

Leave this tomatillo salsa on the chunky side so each ingredient retains its individual texture. Serve with meat, poultry, or seafood or as a dip with fresh vegetables and/or tortilla chips.

6 fresh tomatillos, husked and halved

1 cup water

1 ripe avocado, seeded and peeled

1/2 cup coarsely chopped green onions

1/2 cup loosely packed fresh cilantro leaves

1/3 cup dairy sour cream

1 jalapeño pepper, seeded and coarsely chopped

1/2 teaspoon salt

For Salsa: In a medium saucepan combine tomatillos and water. Bring to boiling; reduce heat. Simmer, uncovered, for 5 to 7 minutes or until soft, stirring occasionally. Remove tomatillos with a slotted spoon; cool slightly. Reserve 2 tablespoons of the cooking liquid. In a food processor bowl or blender container combine tomatillos, the reserved 2 tablespoons cooking liquid, the avocado, green onions, cilantro, sour cream, jalapeño pepper, and salt. Cover and process or blend until combined but still slightly chunky. Transfer to a covered container; chill in the refrigerator for 1 to 24 hours. Serve with grilled meat, poultry, or seafood or as a dip with fresh vegetables and/or tortilla chips. Makes about 2 cups (about 32 tablespoons).

Nutrition Facts per serving: *17 cal., 1 g total fat (0 g sat. fat), 1 mg chol., 35 mg sodium, 1 g carbo., 0 g pro.*

watermelon and jicama salsa

This salsa stands out in a crowd: sweet and juicy watermelon combined with crisp jicama. The addition of jalapeño adds heat to sweet. (Recipe pictured on page 92.)

3   cups chopped, seeded watermelon

1¹/₂ cups thinly sliced, peeled jicama

1   jalapeño pepper, seeded and finely chopped

2   tablespoons chopped green onion

1   tablespoon snipped fresh cilantro or mint

1   tablespoon seasoned rice vinegar

¹/₈ to ¹/₄ teaspoon ground red pepper (optional)

For Salsa: In a medium bowl stir together the watermelon, jicama, jalapeño pepper, green onion, cilantro or mint, vinegar, and red pepper (if desired). If desired, cover and chill in the refrigerator for up to 2 hours, or serve immediately. Serve with grilled chicken, fish, or pork. Makes about 5 cups (about 80 tablespoons).

Nutrition Facts per serving: 7 cal., 0 g total fat (0 g sat. fat), 1 mg chol., 0 mg sodium, 1 g carbo., 1 g pro.

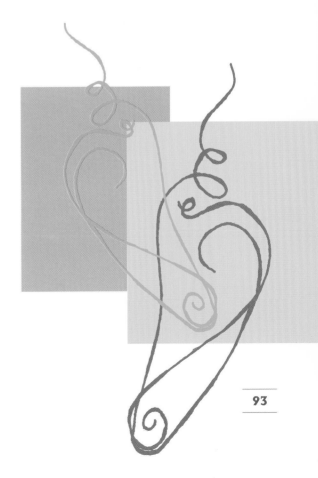

index

Metric Cooking Hints

By making a few conversions, cooks in Australia, Canada, and the United Kingdom can use the recipes in this book with confidence. The charts on this page provide a guide for converting measurements from the U.S. customary system, which is used throughout this book, to the imperial and metric systems. There also is a conversion table for oven temperatures to accommodate the differences in oven calibrations.

Product Differences: Most of the ingredients called for in the recipes in this book are available in English-speaking countries. However, some are known by different names. Here are some common U.S. American ingredients and their possible counterparts:
• Sugar is granulated or castor sugar.
• Powdered sugar is icing sugar.
• All-purpose flour is plain household flour or white flour. When self-rising flour is used in place of all-purpose flour in a recipe that calls for leavening, omit the leavening agent (baking soda or baking powder) and salt.
• Light-colored corn syrup is golden syrup.
• Cornstarch is cornflour.
• Baking soda is bicarbonate of soda.
• Vanilla is vanilla essence.
• Green, red, or yellow sweet peppers are capsicums.
• Golden raisins are sultanas.

Volume and Weight: U.S. Americans traditionally use cup measures for liquid and solid ingredients. The chart, below, shows the approximate imperial and metric equivalents. If you are accustomed to weighing solid ingredients, the following approximate equivalents will help.
• 1 cup butter, castor sugar, or rice = 8 ounces = about 230 grams
• 1 cup flour = 4 ounces = about 115 grams
• 1 cup icing sugar = 5 ounces = about 140 grams

Spoon measures are used for smaller amounts of ingredients. Although the size of the tablespoon varies slightly in different countries, for practical purposes and for recipes in this book, a straight substitution is all that's necessary.

Measurements made using cups or spoons always should be level unless stated otherwise.

EQUIVALENTS: U.S. = AUSTRALIA/U.K.

⅛ teaspoon = 1 ml
¼ teaspoon = 1.25 ml
½ teaspoon = 2.5 ml
1 teaspoon = 5 ml
1 tablespoon = 15 ml
1 fluid ounce = 30 ml
¼ cup = 60 ml
⅓ cup = 80 ml
½ cup = 120 ml
⅔ cup = 160 ml
¾ cup = 180 ml
1 cup = 240 ml
2 cups = 475 ml
1 quart = 1 liter
½ inch = 1.25 cm
1 inch = 2.5 cm

BAKING PAN SIZES

U.S.	Metric
8×1½-inch round baking pan	20×4-cm cake tin
9×1½-inch round baking pan	23×4-cm cake tin
11×7×1½-inch baking pan	28×18×4-cm baking tin
13×9×2-inch baking pan	32×23×5-cm baking tin
2-quart rectangular baking dish	28×18×4-cm baking tin
15×10×1-inch baking pan	38×25.5×2.5-cm baking tin (Swiss roll tin)
9-inch pie plate	22×4- or 23×4-cm pie plate
7- or 8-inch springform pan	18- or 20-cm springform or loose-bottom cake tin
9×5×3-inch loaf pan	23×13×8-cm or 2-pound narrow loaf tin or pâté tin
1½-quart casserole	1.5-liter casserole
2-quart casserole	2-liter casserole

OVEN TEMPERATURE EQUIVALENTS

Fahrenheit Setting	Celsius Setting*	Gas Setting
300°F	150°C	Gas mark 2 (very low)
325°F	170°C	Gas mark 3 (low)
350°F	180°C	Gas mark 4 (moderate)
375°F	190°C	Gas mark 5 (moderately hot)
400°F	200°C	Gas mark 6 (hot)
425°F	220°C	Gas mark 7 (hot)
450°F	230°C	Gas mark 8 (very hot)
475°F	240°C	Gas mark 9 (very hot)
Broil		Grill

*Electric and gas ovens may be calibrated using Celsius. However, for an electric oven, increase the Celsius setting 10 to 20 degrees when cooking above 160°C. For convection or forced-air ovens (gas or electric), lower the temperature setting 10°C when cooking at all heat levels.